THE

Intuition

HANDBOOK

THE
Intuition
HANDBOOK

Access Your Hidden Powers and Transform Your Life

JUDY HALL

ISBN 1-84333-696-0

A catalogue record for this book is available
from the British Library

First published in 2003 by
Vega
64 Brewery Road
London, N7 9NT

A member of **Chrysalis** Books plc

Visit our website at www.chrysalisbooks.co.uk
Printed and bound in Hong Kong

AUTHORS ACKNOWLEDGEMENTS
I would like to acknowledge Thelma Reardon,
Christine Hartley and the many other mentors
who assisted me in opening my own intuition.

DESIGN: Louise Clements
PROJECT MANAGEMENT: Jane Alexander
ILLUSTRATION: Coral Mula
PRODUCTION: Susan Sutterby

contents

CHAPTER one

Out of the blue

'What lies before us and what lies behind us are small matters compared to what lies within us. And when we bring what is within out into the world, miracles happen.'

Henry David Thoreau

awakening to intuition

Developing your own intuition enhances every aspect of your life. You can access hidden knowledge, recognize the correct action to take, become more creative, and instinctively do whatever is right for you.

If you have picked up this book, you may feel in need of guidance but you are unsure where to turn. You may want to improve your business or personal life or to maximize your health and well-being. But before you begin, you need to know who to trust. And you will certainly want to avoid hocus pocus and mumbo jumbo. You may instinctively feel that the answer lies within yourself, and yet do not know how to find it. Intuition is the answer you are seeking.

Intuition is an innate ability we all share. It involves, yet goes beyond, the ordinary five senses. It is a function of consciousness.

Consciousness is one of the last frontiers awaiting exploration. While science knows a great deal about how the brain actually functions – and attributes both mind and consciousness to the brain – it knows little about intuition, despite having studied it for over 150 years.

Most people are intuitive. You may have had the experience of hearing the phone ring and knowing who is on the other end, or of suddenly thinking of someone and having them call. You may be prone to hunches or premonitions. This is intuition at work – as is suddenly knowing which horse to back before a race begins, or which stock is going to rocket in value on the stock market, or which commodity will be in demand. Businesses such as the futures market, or the stock market, rely heavily on intuition. Intellect alone is seldom sufficient. Indeed, the people who are successful in business are often highly intuitive and are not afraid to back a hunch or follow their instincts. But intuition is not only useful in business: it enriches every aspect of your life.

'Vision is the art of seeing things invisible to others.'

Jonathan Swift

TRUSTING TO INTUITION

A classic case of trusting to intuition was demonstrated by a costume designer working on a long-running television soap opera, who felt she needed a break. Friends were horrified that she intended to give up a secure job in an insecure profession. She, however, was not worried. 'When I need it, something will turn up out of the blue,' she asserted. When she returned from a long holiday in the sun she was immediately offered a much better job. It was on a programme called 'Out of The Blue'.

what is intuition?

Intuition is your sixth sense. It is the quiet voice that speaks from inner stillness. A deep knowing that goes beyond the confines of your everyday mind.

An awareness that relies upon gut feeling rather than brain power, intuition is in fact your mind's perceptions rather than your brain's reasoning. It is complementary to intellect but works in a completely different way. Intuition is instantaneous.

Intuition exceeds the ordinary five senses, which is why it is often called extrasensory perception (ESP) or psi. Everyone has it to some extent, and it can be amplified. Much of it occurs at a subliminal level, and a great deal manifests through imagery and feelings rather than words. Bypassing the logical and rational mind, and able to operate separately from the brain, intuition is a source of creativity, insight and new perspectives. Functioning at one level, it takes disparate facts and bits of information, synthesizes them and comes up with an answer that goes way beyond 'the facts'. Operating at another level, intuition pulls things 'out of the blue'. It gives answers and insights that cannot be obtained through ordinary channels. It operates outside time and space. Many of the world's great scientists and inventors, such as Einstein, Edison and Leonardo da Vinci, used intuition in the development of their theories.

DEFINITIONS

'The immediate knowing or learning of
something without the conscious use
of reasoning, instantaneous apperception.'

Webster's Dictionary

'Intuition is that aspect of consciousness
that allows us to see round corners.'

C.G. Jung

'Intuition is the clothing of divine ideas
with the subtlest of form.'

Judy Jacka

'The term intuition does not
denote something contrary to reason,
but something outside of the
province of reason.'

C.G. Jung

'You can think of it as a sneak preview,
like at the movies.'

In.Q.

'The biocomputer within our own mind.'

Jeffrey Mishlove

random intuitions

'The intellect has little to do on the road to discovery. There comes a leap in consciousness, call it intuition or what you will, and the solution comes to you, and you don't know how or why.'

Albert Einstein

'There is an immense ocean over which the mind can sail, upon which the vessel of thought has not yet been launched.'

R. Jefferies

'A characteristic of intuitions is that they are fleeting and, curiously, very easily forgotten …' *[Write them down immediately.]*

Roberto Assagioli

'Intuition allows you to know things as they are.'

Frances E. Vaughan

'Creativeness is the basis of evolution.'

Agni Yoga

'It is by the logic that we prove, but by the intuition that we discover.'

Poincaré

'Imagination is more important than knowledge.'

Albert Einstein

'Intuition is one of the most important abilities we can cultivate.'

Jagdish Parikh

'The intuitive mind tells the thinking mind where to look next … I wake up in the morning wondering what my intuition will toss up to me like gifts from the sea.'

Jonas Salk

how do I know if I'm intuitive?

*If you have had a significant dream or dream in colour, followed
a hunch, a lucky guess, a feeling in your bones, or listened to your heart,
your intuition has made itself known.*

Intuition enables you to take great leaps into the unknown, and find the answers you seek. Everyone is intuitive – it is an innate quality of consciousness. Not everyone consciously responds to their intuition, but it is nevertheless there.

Appraising your intuition

Have you ever said:

- I had a gut feeling.
- I knew that would happen.
- Why didn't I pay attention to that hunch?

- I don't know why, I just know it's so.
- I was just thinking about you.

Do you follow the promptings of your heart? If so, your intuition is already at work, even if you haven't yet recognized it. Take time out now to ponder how you respond to your intuition and hunches.

- When did you last have an intuitive feeling?
- What did it suggest you do?
- Did you act on it?

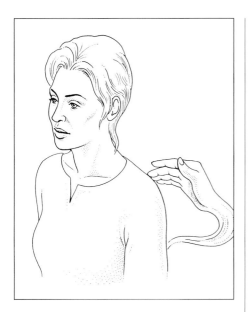

• What was the result?
• How did you feel?
• When did you last ignore an
  intuitive feeling?
• What was the result?
• How did you feel?

You will probably find that acting on your intuition is more productive and successful than ignoring it.

Can I develop my intuition?

Yes. In the same way that you exercise a muscle to build up its strength, your intuition can be strengthened. This is where this book comes in. It is a skilfully structured programme for developing intuition. You can begin work by paying attention to all the times during the day when your intuition tries to speak to you.

• Watch your body's feelings and
  reactions, catch the moment when
  your stomach sinks or you feel
  inexplicably keyed up.
• Notice your first, immediate reaction
  to someone new.
• Notice when you feel good or bad
  about something.

- What impulses do you have?
- Catch the fleeting thoughts that pass through your mind but seem to come from somewhere else.
- Notice the images that pass through your mind whenever your attention wanders.
- Pay attention as you fall asleep or wake up. Make a promise to yourself to act on your intuitions, now.

EXERCISE
How would intuition affect my life?
You can find out what your life would be like with your intuition fully functioning simply by closing your eyes, breathing gently and bringing your awareness away from the outside world and into yourself. Give a big sigh, lift up both your shoulders and, as you let them fall, drop into an altered state of consciousness without thinking about it.

Ask your intuition to show or tell you what life would be like if you worked in partnership together. See how it would flow and weave a harmonious whole. Notice how your body feels.

When you are ready, open your eyes and make a note of your experiences, feelings and sensations.

'Genius results from the miraculous fusion of the human race and the creative universe.'

Sir Ernest Hall, *In Defence of Genius*

INTUITION
People often refer to intuition as

- a hunch
- inspiration
- an instinct
- a gut feeling
- a knowing
- an impulse
- ingenious thought
- a priori knowledge
- creative muse
- premonition
- extrasensory perception
- inner guidance
- a brainwave
- visual thinking
- a lucky guess
- prescience
- a feeling in the bones
- vision

Beginning to programme your intuition

Action follows thought. Affirming that you are intuitive will make it so. Every morning when you wake up, say to yourself: 'Every day in every way I am more intuitive and aware.' Repeat the statement when you go to bed. Remember to phrase your affirmation in the present tense.

different types of intuition

Intuition operates in many ways. At its most simple, it is a hunch or a gut instinct. At its most complex, it can involve precognition and space–time travel.

Abilities that go beyond 'normal' methods of communication are often known as extrasensory perception or psi. The major psi abilities are:

Inner wisdom
Your inner wisdom, often referred to as the voice of the heart or soul, is unlocked by stilling the everyday mind and blocking stimuli from the outer world. In the silence, you access your own knowing.

Telepathy
Telepathy occurs when thoughts, words, or pictures are passed intentionally, or unintentionally, from one mind to another without verbalization or visual clues. Telepathy can operate over vast distances.

Precognition
Moving forward in time to access the future is precognitive intuition.

Retrocognition
Moving backward across time to access knowledge about events in the past is known as retrocognitive intuition.

Remote viewing
The ability for consciousness to leave the

physical body and travel to another place, reporting what is seen there.

Psychokinesis
The ability to move objects by the power of the mind alone uses psi.

Clairvoyance
Clairvoyance literally means 'clear sight'. Information is received through symbols, impressions, thoughts, and pictures. The communication is often with another level of existence, such as the spirits of those who have departed. Clairvoyance can also involve reading the contents of a sealed envelope and such like.

Clairaudience
Clairaudience means hearing clearly. Information may be received through a distinct voice – often heard behind the ear – or by an idea 'popping' into the mind.

Clairsentience
This involves receiving information from a flower or similar object through sensing.

Psychometry
The ability to read the impressions retained by objects or places is known as psychometry. Objects such as a ring may be held in the hand, or impressions gained from buildings.

Channelling
Channelling used to be called trance. A spirit or being who is no longer on earth (or who, it is claimed, is extraterrestrial) communicates through the medium of a living person using their voice or hand.

Automatic writing
In automatic writing it feels as though something outside oneself is doing the writing. Words appear without thought.

how does intuition communicate?

Research carried out in the 1960s showed that at least half of spontaneous ESP experiences occurred during dreams, and in 1970 it was concluded that 70 per cent of such cases involved imagery of one kind or another.

Imagery is the language of intuition. Images are constantly passing through our minds – the trick is to recognize those that have a message for us.

There is, however, no one right way to access intuition. One person will 'hear an inner voice', another will 'see a mind picture', while a third will 'feel it' or 'get a sense about it', yet another will 'just know' and someone else will 'get it in the gut'. This book will help you to identify which is 'your way'. The exercises will guide you through that process, and teach you how to develop your intuition into a highly skilled, reliable tool. Each section is accompanied by practical exercises to help you understand how your own intuition works and how to tone up and develop the sixth sense.

If your intuition functions through your body, it is kinaesthetic. Kinaesthetic awareness covers sensing with your hands, feelings in your bones, gut feelings, head prickling or the hairs on your arms standing up. It is what makes dowsing work. Minute twitches in your muscles translate into a pendulum swinging, a rod moving or your finger sticking. You may also have a different kind of feeling, something which involves 'just knowing'.

You aren't quite sure how you came to know, but you do indeed know.

Intuition can function at a mental or psychic level. If it is mental, a thought that is not yours floats into your head and has the answer to a question, or the information you need. If it is psychic, you may clearly hear a voice speaking to you, or you may get a mind picture projected onto an inner screen. Intuition may come when you write without thinking first, or when you enter a creative reverie or dream state. By trying out the different methods, you can develop a range of intuitive skills for a variety of situations. Intuition is a valuable tool. It may even save your life.

Is intuition always accurate?

Untutored intuition is not an accurate process, which is why intuition needs to be honed and developed to make it more reliable. Common sense, combined with the passage of time, is the most reliable tool for assessing accuracy. If in doubt, place the information in a mental filing cabinet and reassess it periodically.

'Intuition … can be activated following the general principle that attention and interest foster their manifestations.'

Roberto Assagioli, *Psychosynthesis Manual*

what facilitates intuition?

Intuitive information may be received through the physical body or the subtle senses in various ways, depending on the varying sensitivity of the individual. It is affected by various factors.

Receiving information
- Hearing *(aural)*
- Seeing *(visual)*
- Sensing *(kinaesthetic)*
- Feeling *(kinaesthetic)*
- Knowing *(kinaesthetic)*
- Smelling *(kinaesthetic)*

Crucial factors
Research has shown that there are ten crucial factors that enhance intuition:
- An open mind
- Belief
- Desire
- Intention
- Expectation
- A positive attitude
- The ability to move out of everyday awareness
- Trust
- Common sense
- Willingness to take risks

An open mind
Keeping an open mind is essential. Do not explore your intuition with a cynical and critical attitude: intuition is a subjective state and, if you try to remain objective during experiments, you will not access the subliminal perceptions on

which intuition is based. A closed mind shuts out intuition and, even if your intuition starts screaming at you, you won't hear it. An open mind does not mean a gullible mind. An open mind looks at the evidence, assesses it logically and dispassionately, and accepts or rejects it on the basis of what is.

Belief

Whether or not you believe in intuition will affect whether your intuition can function. If you don't believe in intuition, for you it will not exist. Intuition, which is a delicate and sensitive force, disappears under the weight of disbelief. When you first explore intuition, you are in

SMELL AND INTUITION

The olfactory sense is often overlooked in intuitive sensing and yet it is a powerful and evocative form of communication. As metaphysical abilities develop, it is common for certain aromas to be perceived even though they are not present in the physical world. Incense often wafts through the air, or perfumes such as lavender or rose suffuse your immediate environment. Smells that belong to a certain location can alert your attention to events occurring there, even if you are many miles away. Intuition can be enhanced by burning suitable fragrances or joss sticks, and some oils, such as sandalwood, myrrh and frankincense, have been prized over millennia for their consciousness-lifting effects.

something of a catch-22 situation. If you have not experienced it for yourself, someone else telling you will almost certainly not lead to belief. You need to have the experience. But even if you do have the experience, you may try to explain it away. Most people who have one or two unexplained things in their life are apt to say: 'But it could all be my imagination.' Yes, it could. But if such things prove themselves over and over again to be true and reliable, it might be more sensible to start believing in them.

If you believe you are intuitive, you will find something magical happens. Your intuition will be so pleased it has caught your attention at last, it will work extra hard on your behalf.

Desire

Desire is a powerful force and an excellent motivator. You must desire an outcome. If you are indifferent as to whether you succeed or not, your intuition will be dulled. If you really want to succeed, your chances of success increase.

'Within every single one of us lies well upon well of spiritual peace untapped, of spiritual intelligence untouched.'

Dr Paul Brunton, *The Secret Path*

Intention

Similarly, you need to have the intention that you will succeed. Intention is what shamans have used in their work for thousands of years. It focuses the will and sets things in motion. If you hold an intent strongly and clearly, it will manifest.

Expectation

If you are to utilize your intuition fully, you must expect that it will work. Doubts poison intuition. Expecting that you will quickly master an exercise, having positive thoughts and attitudes, allows intuition to flourish. The expectation that you will receive an answer sets receiving that answer in motion. You may need a little patience, but the answer will come.

A positive attitude

If you constantly undermine yourself by believing that you are not good enough, not capable enough, too stupid and so on, you will consistently fail. If you have negative thoughts, you will manifest what you most fear. On the other hand, maintaining positive thoughts and attitudes can overcome even the most difficult handicap.

For instance, as a child, Albert Einstein was dyslexic and had problems with his speech. He initially flunked the entrance exam for college and, when he finally graduated, he could only find a dead-end job in the Swiss patents office. However, he managed to overcome all these problems and was later regarded as a genius. In 1905, at the age of 27, he published his theory of relativity – which had come to him in a five-second flash but taken ten years to decode the implications. Maintaining a positive attitude enhances your intuition and helps you attain your goals.

The ability to move out of everyday awareness

Intuition functions best in a state of heightened awareness and low sensory input. This is achieved by withdrawing your awareness from the outside world and bringing attention into your self to contact the source of your intuition. Optimum conditions for heightened awareness are created by stimulating alpha and theta waves in the brain. These signal that you are relaxed and in a receptive state. With a little practise, you can learn to enter this state quite quickly.

Trust

You need to trust yourself, the guidance you receive and the process. However, this trust is not a gullible state where you take everything you are given and assume that it is absolute truth. You also need to use your common sense and your ability to discriminate.

Common sense

Some people believe that intuition is the antithesis of common sense. But this is not true. Your common sense will help you to keep your feet on the ground – and some people's 'common sense' is actually extremely intuitive. But too much common sense can be a handicap. It can lead to questioning everything and accepting nothing because it does not follow the known laws of logic or science. However, applying your common sense to whatever your intuition urges you to do can be a very useful process. If you get into the habit of checking things out with an open mind while still trusting the process, your common sense will be harnessed to your intuition instead of creating mental conflict.

A willingness to take risks

Speaking from your intuition, certainly in the initial stages, may feel threatening, specially if you lack confidence in yourself. The willingness to take a risk is vital if you are to expand your intuition. Without that ability, you may never begin the exercises. And, if you are working with a group, the ability to take a risk – especially the risk of not getting it right first time – is of paramount importance.

'The state of awareness of visions is not one in which we are either remembering or perceiving. It is rather a level of consciousness at which we experience visions within ourselves.'

Oscar Kokoschka

what aids intuitive abilities?

*Scientific research has shown that altered states of consciousness
and deep relaxation, where the brain produces alpha and theta wavelengths,
help intuition to function efficiently.*

In laboratory tests, dreaming, hypnosis and meditation have been proved to be conducive to psi and intuitive abilities. A survey of research in 1976 showed that experiments performed with the subject in an altered state had a 56 per cent success rate compared to a chance expectation of only 5 per cent – which is exactly what spiritual masters have known for thousands of years.

Eastern mysticism

Traditionally, aspiring spiritual seekers in the East were taught how to enter a state of consciousness in which there was no clear boundary around oneself and in which sensory input was at a minimum. They sought the elusive goal of 'no mind', but one of the side effects was an increase in extrasensory perception and visionary experiences.

Altered consciousness

Western mystics are familiar with the same state. In the thirteenth century, Meister Eckhart wrote: 'I assert that in heaven all is in all and all is one and all is ours … Thus spirit is in spirit.' For him the goal of religion was to realize the 'God-within' and once this union was achieved, there were no boundaries between oneself and God.

With a little application, you too can utilize altered states of consciousness to access your intuition. Learning to relax is a crucial first step, and as you work through this book you will gradually build up other skills, such as visualization and sensing subtle signals. Relaxation is a little like self-hypnosis. Many of the exercises take you into a state similar to light hypnosis – which means you enter an altered and heightened state of awareness, which facilitates the working of your intuition.

Behavioural psychologists have proved time and time again that if an action is reinforced, it becomes habitual. So, exercising your intuition strengthens it. The more you listen to your inner voice or open your third eye, the more intuitive you will become.

ENHANCING INTUITION

Major factors confirmed in research were:

- Muscle relaxation
- Reduced sensory input
- Cortical arousal (that is, the subject remained attentive)
- Spontaneous mental processes, especially imagery
- A goal or a need to communicate

In addition, consciousness-raising agents such as incense, certain hallucinogenic substances and music can play a powerful part in enhancing intuition. Entering a relaxed state while remaining alert and attentive induces intuition.

CHAPTER two

Does intuition exist?

'There exists, already, sufficient evidence for the existence of [psi] phenomena which are incompatible with the known laws of physics.'

John Beloff, Honorary Fellow of Department of Psychology, Edinburgh

testing, testing

Parapsychology studies the existence of psi or ESP. The more research can 'prove' the existence of abilities beyond the normal senses, the more potential there is for acceptance of an intuitive faculty.

When astronaut Edgar Mitchell went to the moon, he took with him a pack of Zener cards (see illustration on page 37). He used the cards to conduct telepathy experiments with people back on earth. The results were such that, when he left the Space Program, he turned to the study of metaphysics and parapsychology, and in 1973 he founded the Institute for Noetic Sciences.

American Professor Charles Honorton, former director of the American Parapsychological Association, in an extensive review of 50 years' research, pointed out that while psi research has consistently failed to find a physical basis for the phenomenon, it has shown that, so far as can be ascertained in the light of current knowledge, it has a distinctly psychological basis. That is, it is a function of mind.

The inner censor

At any given moment your brain is receiving and processing zillions of bits of information. If you paid attention to all of these, life would be an incomprehensible jumble. You would be in sensory overload. So, your perceptions are censored before you become aware of them. Your brain gives you the information it thinks you need. But your intuitive mind is aware of much more – and passes this before your inner eye. It is this mind and inner eye (or ear) link that is called intuition.

The corner of your eye may have noticed something. Say, for instance, it has seen a patch of wetness on your car tyre that looks as though a dog has sprayed against it. Your brain has not considered this important because it does not know that this could signify a serious problem with the brakes. But your mind is aware. So it gives you a dream in which your brakes fail. If you are wise, following such a dream you would have your brakes thoroughly checked.

Major research work has been done on telepathy and remote viewing. Remote viewing, while strictly speaking not intuitive, shows that consciousness can exist outside the body – and that it is not dependent on the brain. Consciousness is the part of human experience that science has been slow to catch on to. Researchers are usually more concerned with proving that consciousness is a function of the brain than exploring the enormous possibilities that consciousness beyond the brain opens up.

'Parapsychology is important because everywhere it lurks just below the surface.'

C.G. Jung

parapsychology

Parapsychology is: 'The study of interactions between living systems and their environment . . . characterized by the acquisition of information from the outside world under conditions prohibiting involvement of known physiological receptors.'

In 1982 the Dean of the School of Engineering and Applied Science at Princeton University had this to say about psychical research:

'Although a variety of so-called psychic phenomena have attracted man's attention throughout recorded history, organized scholarly effort to comprehend such effects is just one century old, and systematic academic research roughly half that age. Over recent years, a sizeable spectrum of evidence has been brought forth from reputable laboratories in several disciplines to suggest that at times human consciousness can acquire information inaccessible by any known physical mechanism.'

(R.G. Jahn, Princeton)

And it has also been pointed out that: 'There have been numerous replications of all the principal psi phenomena, as the many published meta-analyses testify. It remains true, nevertheless, that one can never depend on a particular psi effect showing up exactly when and where it may be required … Indeed, all our experience so far points to the fact that psi is, for whatever reason, inherently elusive and evasive …'

(John Beloff, *Thinking Beyond the Brain*)

It is clear from research that:

'The psi factor in nature is apparently not constrained by the laws of physics, chemistry, and biology, at least as they are understood today.'

(Michael Grosso, Chair of Philosophy and Religion, New Jersey City University)

Scientific limitations

Nevertheless, it is still true that:

'We may safely predict that it will be the timidity of our hypotheses, and not their extravagance, that will provoke the derision of posterity.'

(Professor H.H. Price, Psychic Researcher, 1950s)

It may well be that science has been asking the wrong questions, or looking at the whole question of intuition from an erroneous perspective. As Michael Grosso succinctly puts it:

'What's lacking, in my opinion, is knowledge that is immediate, intuitive.'

Zener symbols

Scientists themselves would perhaps be better employed exploring their own intuitive abilities rather than seeking to understand intuition in someone else.

metaphysical research

*For over 150 years, scientists have been trying to prove –
or more often disprove – metaphysical abilities (more usually known
as psi in scientific research circles).*

From the middle of the 19th century, in Victorian England, The Ghost Society at Cambridge University, the Phantasmological Society at Oxford and, in 1871, The London Dialectical Society, looked into 'subjects which are ostracized elsewhere, especially those of a meta-physical, religious, social or political nature'.

Early research

Such societies did not achieve much in the way of convincing research, but in January 1882 the Society for Psychical Research was formed to put psi under the searchlight of rigorous scientific research. Founder members included Henry Sidgwick (a Fellow of Trinity College, Cambridge), Frederic Myers, Lord Rayleigh, Sir William Barrett (Professor of Physics at the Royal College of Science, Dublin), the physicist Sir William Crookes and Gerald Balfour, a Cabinet minister. The society, which still exists today, amassed an enormous body of evidence in response to their first question, 'Does psi exist?'. The answer was a resounding 'Yes!'. Later they turned their attention to explaining how it functioned. The results of well over 100 years of the Society's research are meticulously recorded in their Proceedings. They make convincing reading.

Research in the United States

America, too, undertook psychical research. In 1927 Duke University was established at Durham, North Carolina, and the head of the psychology department was the British psychologist Professor William McDougall (a former Harvard professor). McDougall was a member of the Society for Psychical Research and he soon set up a research facility at Duke under J.B. Rhine.

Rhine began by testing telepathy with specially designed Zener cards. The cards were in suits of five simple shapes: a cross, a square, a circle, a five-pointed star and three parallel wavy lines. Each pack contained five of each card. Researchers would use a 'sender' and a 'receiver'. The sender would concentrate on the card and the receiver would draw a symbol. Results would be compared with random chance. If the receiver scored significantly more than chance, it would constitute success.

A scientific fact

When Rhine's first published his report on ESP in 1934, he aroused enormous hostility in his scientific colleagues because he felt, after due consideration, that psi was a scientific fact, even if science could not yet explain how it functioned. Almost three quarters of a century later, the position is little changed.

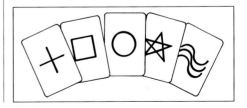

more recent research

As scientific research developed in the second half of the 20th century, the process of the intuitive state was examined, rather than the fact that it existed.

Researchers explored the states that were conducive to psi and identified factors that affected its operation, such as emotions, the environment and interaction between researchers and participants. They found that by creating states that were conducive to intuition, such as dreaming, meditation and hypnosis, the success rate increased to 56 per cent, compared with a chance factor of just 5 per cent. It is easy to prove that intuition happens at rates well above random chance, but it has proved much more difficult to explain the why and the how of it.

Problems facing researchers

While there is an enormous body of evidence from such early pioneers as the Society for Psychical Research, J.B. Rhine and later researchers, much of the evidence for psi and intuition is still anecdotal rather than empirical – that is, it is not repeatable in a laboratory under strict conditions. (This may well be because strict laboratory conditions induce an atmosphere that is antithetical to intuition.) Scientific criteria insist that experimental results be consistent and replicable with an incident of the phenomena well above chance. Unfortunately, the energy with which they are experimenting is temperamental and elusive, and far from replicable. It behaves strangely and does not follow any known scientific laws. It does not adhere to time – people exercising psi apparently move forward and backward in time, or out of it altogether.

Telepathy experiments

In more than one set of telepathy experiments, the person 'receiving' anticipated the object before it was 'sent' – precognition. At first the experimenters believed that way below chance had been scored. Only when the results were reconsidered was it recognized that the 'receiver' had been one symbol ahead of what was sent.

In reporting his own interim results in 1982, and having surveyed over 50 years of psychical research by other highly respected institutions, Professor R.G. Jahn, Dean of the School of Engineering and Applied Science at Princeton University, commented that while metaphysical phenomena were difficult to replicate consistently, nevertheless in some cases results were well above random

'Human Beings are gods hidden from themselves.'

Ben Okri, *The Famished Road*

chance – particularly in the fields of remote viewing and psychokinesis (the ability to move objects by the power of the mind alone). His report summed up the difficulties: 'Once the illegitimate research and invalid criticism have been set aside, the remaining accumulated evidence of psychic phenomena comprises an array of experimental observations, obtained under reasonable protocols in a variety of scholarly disciplines, which compound to a philosophical dilemma. On one hand, effects inexplicable in terms of established scientific theory, yet having numerous common characteristics, are frequently and widely observed; on the other hand, these effects have so far proven qualitatively and quantitatively irreplicable, in the strict scientific sense, and appear to be sensitive to a variety of psychological and environmental factors that are difficult to specify, let alone control.'

Intuition and metaphysical abilities are particularly susceptible to 'human factors'. The state of mind of a subject affects the outcome. The weather and other factors can affect state of mind. If someone is bored, too hot or too cold, or tired, the results will be poor.

Intention and expectation

The British healer Matthew Manning was extensively tested in the 1970s. He says that if the testing involved healing, his enthusiasm and intention was engaged and the tests worked well. But if the test was on telepathy or psychokinesis, he quickly became bored, lost intention, and the results tailed off. For him, intention and expectation are vital in successful metaphysical work. He intends and expects that something will occur, and it does.

There is another difficulty. Science has proved that observers interfere with the results of experiments by being there. In the metaphysical field, a cynical observer who does not believe that something is possible will adversely affect the outcome. In college, a fellow student and I were looking at the incidence of chance. The experiment involved throwing two coins to see whether they would fall as heads or tails, matched or odd pairs. My fellow student and I happened to be sitting in a spiritual development group at the time, but we were in no way trying to influence the fall of the coins – at least not consciously. However, our first throw was two heads, so was our second, our third and our fourth.

By the time we got to our twenty-third-in-a-row throw of heads, the 'observer' who was recording the results was encouraging us, somewhat loudly – which brought the mathematics tutor over. 'Impossible,' she said firmly. 'Throw again.' We did, but for the rest of the session two heads did not appear together despite throwing the coin a great many times. Her assessment of the situation: 'A fluke, sometimes it goes like that.' Her mathematical mind put everything down to random chance. She could not comprehend either intuition or psi experiences. They existed outside her scientific framework.

Intuition and metaphysical abilities are particularly susceptible to 'human factors'

remote viewing

One of the most well-known ways in which consciousness can operate outside the body is through remote viewing, the ability to leave your body and visit far-flung parts of the earth.

As Michael Talbot succinctly put it: 'There is evidence that we are ultimately no more bound by space than we are by time.'

Remote viewing is a subject that arouses great controversy. It is also known as journeying out of the body, out-of-body experience (OOBE) and etheric or astral travel. Strictly speaking it is a metaphysical ability rather than an intuitive one, but it does help you to hone your intuition and it certainly demonstrates that consciousness can operate away from the body. Until you experience a journey out of your body, it is possible to believe it is all a delusion. But once you have mastered it, you cannot doubt that it is real. Remote viewing uses the ability of consciousness to leave the physical body behind and travel to a distant place, bringing back an accurate report of what is seen or heard.

Remote viewing, near-death experiences and dreams

Many people who undergo near-death experiences (NDEs) report some degree of remote viewing. They correctly describe events that go on out of the sight or hearing of the body they leave behind as they 'die'. Such information is particularly significant when it comes from someone who, in life, was blind and could not under ordinary circumstances be able to know such things as the colour of a nurse's hair or what a doctor was wearing, for instance, and yet there have been detailed reports of such incidents. Complex resuscitation or other procedures are commonly described. People who have had spontaneous out-of-body events frequently obtain information that they simply could not perceive in any other way.

A number of people have out-of-body experiences as part of their dreams.

FAMOUS OUT-OF-BODY JOURNEYS

Remote viewing and out-of-body experiences are nothing new. Most of the great religious figures had at least one such experience. Christ was taken by the devil to the Holy City and set on the parapet of the temple as part of his temptation (Matthew 4:5), St Paul tells us in Corinthians II 12:2–4 that he knew 'a man [himself] in Christ who, fourteen years ago, was caught up – whether still in the body or out of the body, I do not know … right into the third heaven, into paradise and heard words so secret that human lips may not repeat them.' This was part of his conversion experience, his 'Road to Damascus'. Mohammed made his night journey to Jerusalem in a similar fashion. Much earlier, the Hindu Sutras of Patanjali taught the practice of projection out of the body.

Flying dreams may show an aptitude for remote viewing, for instance. The jolt felt immediately before waking can be caused by consciousness returning to the body. It only takes a little effort to extend your awareness into recognition of being out of your body, and to direct your consciousness to view remote objects or places. Orthodox science has been attempting to

replicate these experiences satisfactorily – and repeatedly – for the last 50 years or so.

Science and remote viewing
In 1973 the CIA started Project Scanate (later called Star Gate). It arose from Hal Puthoff's and Russell Targ's work at Stanford Research Institute. They found that some of their subjects, when given the geographical coordinates of a place, could describe what was located there. The term 'remote viewing' was coined by one of their star performers, Ingo Swann.

In the early experiments carried out by Scanate, two remote viewers are reported to have correctly identified a site in West Virginia as a secret underground facility, accurately describing it both above and below ground. One of the viewers brought back secret code words and the names of personnel. The data was so accurate it set off a security investigation.

'What the mind of man can conceive and believe, it can achieve.'

Napoleon Hill

In 1981 the Committee on Science and Technology of the US House of Representatives called for a serious assessment of research into para-psychology and what it called 'the physics of consciousness'. As the report explained: 'In the area of national defence, there are obvious implications of one's ability to identify distant sites and affect sensitive instruments or other humans. A general recognition of the degree of inter-connectiveness of mind could have far-reaching social and political implications for this Nation and the World.'

In 1995 the CIA undertook an evaluation of 24 years of research by project Star Gate on using ESP in defence work. Much of the work of the project was so secret that it could not be examined – around 80,000 report pages were withheld. Nevertheless, the statistician from the University of California, Professor Jessica Utts, who sat on the committee declared: 'The statistical results were so overwhelming that results that extreme or more so would occur only about once in every 10 to the 20th such instances if chance alone is the explanation.' She went on to say that: 'There is little benefit to continuing experiments designed to offer proof, since there is little more to be offered to anyone who does not accept the current collection of data . . . anomalous cognition is possible and has been demonstrated. This conclusion is not based on belief, but rather on commonly accepted scientific criteria.' All this despite the fact that the enquiry apparently determined that the work had not been worthwhile!

Disputed results

A critic of the enquiry, Dr Edwin May, a researcher from Stanford who furnished evidence to the committee but who was convinced that it was set up to fail, insists 'the evaluation domain of the research and particularly the operations were restricted to preclude positive findings,' and asks: 'How is it that the CIA and AIR could not find compelling evidence for operational utility of anomalous cognition?' He supplies his own succinct answer: 'They clearly chose not to look.' [The reports can be found on <http://anson.ucdavis.edu/-utts>.]

Useful work

A typical example of the work carried out by remote viewers was that by Gary Langford and Joe McMoneagle in 1981. Langford described a blue van with unusual white markings on the sides, driven by 'Latin-looking terrorists'. In the van was a high-ranking US official. Langford was, however, aware that he was looking forward in time (precognition). Within a few days, Italian Red Brigade terrorists had kidnapped James Dozier, a NATO General – in a blue van with white markings. McMoneagle took a remote journey to Padua, Italy. He drew a second-floor apartment above a shop with a distinctive frontage, and a street map. When the Italian police stormed the apartment where the General was being held, it was above a shop with exactly the same front as McMoneagle had drawn.

Researchers have become more and more inventive as they seek to understand the phenomena. They have shielded targets, and subjects, with Faraday cages and ganzfeld fields to rule out any type of electrical conductivity, magnetism or radio waves, and have even sent remote viewers down in a submarine because sea water shields against all but the lowest frequencies of the electro-magnetic spectrum.

'Double blind' experiments were set up so that the researcher working with the remote viewer did not know the target. In one such experiment, for local targets, a random number generator would be used to pick out one of 100 ready-prepared sealed orders. These orders would be handed

to a target team who would travel to the site. Both viewer in the laboratory and target team at the site would record impressions by taping a description or drawing for about 15 minutes.

Independent assessment

The experimenter working with the viewer would question him as to his impressions. As the experimenter did not know the target, he could not influence the results. The results would be assessed by an independent judge who visited the targets. The judge had to match a report with the correct location. Seven out of nine targets and reports were correctly matched.

While the descriptions were generally accurate, there would be minor inaccuracies. A park with two swimming pools were, for instance, incorrectly described as a water treatment plant although the pools had been accurately described as to shape (one circular, one rectangular) and the approximate dimensions noted. This led to the researchers concluding that remote viewing uses the non-analytic part of the brain's cognitive apparatus.

This is the part used in spatial and other holistic processing, rather than the analytic part of the brain, which is verbal. In other words, intuition is a right-brain function, more related to images than words. Targets have been successfully identified over distances of at least 10,000 km, although some remote viewers have travelled much further.

Psychic spies

Clearly the ability to remote view has security implications – it is silent and does not show up on conventional surveillance scanners and is, therefore, undetectable. A remote viewer can

A JOURNEY THROUGH SPACE

In the 1970s, the American Ingo Swann reported a remote-viewing journey to Jupiter, to which a space probe was being sent. Swann began his description with the words: 'There is a big planet with stripes, I hope it is Jupiter.' He described a thick hydrogen mantle and bands of glittering 'crystals' close into the atmosphere. However, the fact that he saw a ring around rather than the known bands on the planet made observers wonder if he had mistakenly targeted Saturn. But when the space probe arrived six years later, it confirmed everything that Swann had seen. The rings were clearly visible on photographs and the atmosphere was largely liquid hydrogen. It also confirmed that the moons of Jupiter were as described by satirist Jonathan Swift, author of *Gulliver's Travels*, some two centuries earlier. Ingo Swann's ability was a natural one. It manifested at the age of three. During a tonsillectomy, he was anaesthetized and apparently unconscious. However, when he recovered he described the operation in great detail. When he was older, he trained himself to leave his body at will. As an adult he was tested extensively by the Stanford Research Institute in California.

function as a 'spy satellite' but with the advantage that a 'psychic spy' can go in much closer. Both the CIA in America and the KGB in Russia had experimental training programmes for remote viewing. Much of the information remains classified. Nevertheless, several accounts by CIA psychics are published alongside many university research reports.

The CIA in the USSR

One of these reports tells of a remote journey to a remote corner of Kazakstan in 1973. The CIA were concerned that the Russian base there was an underground atomic testing station. The coordinates were given to Hal Puthoff of Project Scanate. One of his remote viewers, Pat Price, immediately began to sketch several objects, including a huge crane which moved on wheels higher than a man, and industrial buildings. This coincided with a CIA sketch already obtained by more conventional spying techniques. Price went on to describe an enormous hall in which workers were assembling giant metal spheres by a new welding technique. A US spy satellite later took pictures of giant spheres with the exact diameter given by Price – which were subsequently found to have been created by an innovative weld.

Classified information

The report was immediately stamped 'exempt from automatic declassification' which meant that the results could not be made public even after 20 years. Russell Targ, however, successfully applied for its release in 1994, 21 years later, and said: 'Thus, I am finally able to thank the CIA for their generous support of this research without going to prison for referring to ESP and the CIA in the same sentence.'

your power to remote view

Remote viewing is a subject that arouses great controversy.
Until you experience it, it is possible to believe it is all a delusion.
But once you have mastered it, you cannot doubt that it is real.

Trained OOBE practitioners make epic journeys to planets or invisibly invade the Kremlin, but you too can develop OOBE ability through a simple exercise. You will need the assistance of a friend, at least in the initial stages.

You may like to return to the following exercise when you have worked through this book, developed control over your abilities and learned to shield yourself if necessary, but unexpected success now may encourage you to go further.

The exercise

The exercise can be memorized or taped but, in the initial stages at least, it is helpful to have a friend read the instructions, pausing to allow you to carry them out. This ensures that there is someone to guide you back to your body at the end of the

'Intuition is the creative advance toward reality.'

Roberto Assagioli

exercise until this becomes an automatic process. With a little practice, you will be able to carry out the relaxation technique and maintain your alertness and awareness. If you find you fall asleep, you may prefer to do the exercise sitting up. The instructions suggest placing an object high up because most people find themselves below the ceiling when they take a remote-viewing journey. If your way is to be closer to the floor, adjust the placement the next time you do the experiment.

Remote-viewing experiment

Ask your friend to place an object, unknown to you, in a room reasonably close to your bedroom, above head height – agree on the positioning before you start the experiment but make sure it is not somewhere where you can accidentally glimpse the object (see illustration on the right for appropriate positioning). A locked

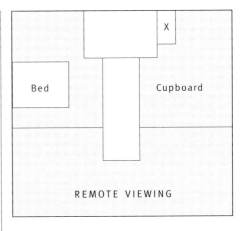

room to which your friend holds the key is ideal but initially doors should be left open until you have learned to bilocate your consciousness instantly – and to recognize that during remote viewing you can pass through apparently solid objects such as doors. The friend should, initially, choose something simple and bright and colourful, like a ball or box, but should not tell you what it is.

Deeper Relaxation

The greater the state of relaxation you can induce, the more success you will achieve. Remain calm and unaffected by the seemingly impossible. It is perfectly possible to walk through walls.

EXERCISE
Basic relaxation technique

Lie down on your bed and allow yourself to relax. Breathe deeply and evenly. As you breathe in, close your eyes. As you breathe out, open them. Do this ten times and then leave your eyes closed. By this time your eyelids will be feeling heavy and relaxed. Allow this feeling to spread all over your face. If you are aware of any tension, raise and lower your eyebrows two or three times. Let the feeling of relaxation flow down through your shoulders and arms. If the shoulders feel stiff, raise and lower each one in turn. If your hands are tense, clench them and then let them lie softly by your side. Allow the feeling to pass down through your chest, your abdomen and into your legs and feet. By this time, you will be feeling totally relaxed. Remind yourself to stay alert and aware while deeply relaxed. (If your body starts vibrating or feels like it is rolling from side to side, this is a good sign that your consciousness is detaching.)

Leaving your body

Slowly and gently withdraw your awareness from your body and let it focus on the centre of your forehead, between and slightly above the eyebrows. Become aware that something is tugging gently at this point, let it pull your consciousness up and out. Soon you will find yourself floating above your body. You can turn and look down to see it lying on the bed below you. You will notice that there is a cord connecting your body with you as you float above the bed. This cord – which often shows itself as a pulsating silver line – goes from the forehead of your body to the subtle body, acting as a vehicle for your awareness. You can use it to return to your physical body at any time by imagining yourself being 'reeled in' by your body. (If this is the first time you are aware of leaving your body, you might like to practise this by moving forward a little way and letting yourself be reeled back toward your body until you are quite comfortable with the process.)

Now make your way from the bed across to the door of your room. You will notice that in this unembodied form, you can pass through solid objects as easily as through the air. So, you will not need to open doors that are closed. Turn (right or left) out of the door and make your way down the hallway to the next room. Let your awareness pass through this door as well. Move over to where you know the object has been placed. Look at it carefully and notice its shape, colour and texture. Is there anything at all unusual about it? Is there anything else lying close to it?

'Experience is capable of teaching us things that words or symbolisms cannot.'

Professor Brian Josephson, Physicist, Cambridge University

Returning to your body

Turn and make your way back to your room, letting the 'line' gently pull you back to your body. Let your consciousness flow back into your body. Settle yourself comfortably and become aware of your body once more. Take your attention from the top of your head, down to your hands, through your chest and abdomen and down your legs to your feet, and back

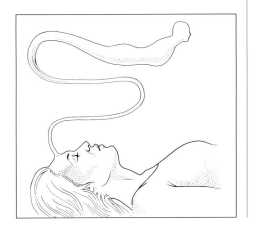

up again. Run your hands down your body to make sure that you are firmly anchored in your body. Give yourself a few moments to adjust and slowly sit up. Put both your feet firmly on the floor.

Immediately write down what you saw in as much detail as possible and have a hot drink before you discuss the experiment with your friend.

Expanding your remote-viewing technique

As you improve with practice, you can vary the placement and the object. You can also have some fun by switching things around so that you know what object you are seeing but do not know which room it is in. Gradually move the object further away. Remote viewing 'hide and seek' entails your friend placing several objects all over the house and challenging you to find, and remember, them all. This is both fun to do and a helpful exercise.

When you are completely confident that you can return to your body at will and that you have total control over the process, you can begin to take longer journeys, programming-in that the shift of awareness be instantaneous by saying, as you leave your body, 'I now instantly go to ….'

When you decide to undertake any kind of remote viewing journey, do remember that it is extremely important to respect other people's privacy as otherwise the ability can rebound on you – no metaphysical power can be misused with impunity!

Always make comprehensive notes of your remote viewing journeys in your Intuition Journal as this may build into a bigger picture over time. Or, you can then continue as in lucid dreaming (page 292).

EXERCISE
Dealing with an unexpected out-of-body experience

As you open up your metaphysical abilities you may find yourself having an unexpected out-of-body experience. This can occur during sleep, meditation

You will notice that there is a cord connecting your body with you as you float above the bed.

or at any other moment. Once you know how to deal with this, it is quite simple to return to your body.

• Stay calm and do not panic.
• Decide whether you want to continue the experience or return to your body.
• The easiest way to return to your body is to think yourself back. Give yourself the instruction 'Back to my body, now' and picture yourself melting back into your body. This usually works instantaneously. If it does not, 'reel yourself in' via the silver cord. Picture this retracting into your body and pulling you back at the same time.

If these experiences occur frequently, wearing a piece of hematite helps you to stay in your body. A combination of the Australian Bush Flower Essences Fringed Violet, Crowea and Sundew will also keep you grounded.

near-death experiences

An NDE occurs when someone, apparently, dies and returns to life to report the experience of a continuation of awareness. NDEs occur across all ages and cultures, and have been reported for over 5,000 years.

There are now many thousands of reports of near-death experiences (NDEs) but when I had an NDE 35 years ago, I had no idea that I was entering into an experience reported throughout all cultures over thousands of years. Indeed, it wasn't until ten years had passed that I learned my experience had a name. It took me into spiritual development and regression work at a time when there were few people doing it and, as I shared my experience, I heard many reports of NDEs, all of which contained several of the components of what I came to see as the classic NDE.

The experience did not so much trigger my intuition as intensify it to a pitch I could not resist. As a child, I had quickly realized that I saw and heard things to

A soul may be offered a choice or is told to return as it is not yet time.

which most of the adults around me were oblivious – and some which they preferred to keep hidden. I learned, as so many children do, to keep quiet. I suppressed my abilities. My NDE brought them bursting to the surface again.

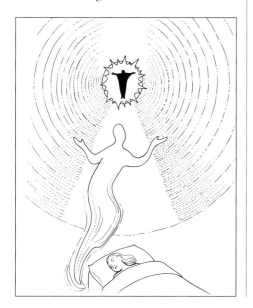

CLASSIC NEAR-DEATH EXPERIENCE

- Consciousness leaves the body suddenly and without premeditation, the body is typically unconscious or 'dead' but may be in a heightened state of awareness.
- Deep feeling of peace.
- Soul passes up a tunnel of light.
- The soul is met by a being of light radiating love, often a religious figure.
- Deceased relatives may appear.
- Soul hears beautiful music and sees wondrous surroundings.
- Soul undergoes a Life Review, an intense experience.
- Soul identifies on-going lessons and processes.
- Soul may be offered a choice or told to return as it is not yet time.

science and NDEs

Dr Peter Fenwick investigated over 300 NDEs to establish whether an NDE was anything more than a 'trick played on us by a brain disordered by drugs, pain or sickness'.

A much respected neuro–psychiatrist, Dr Fenwick also wanted to explore what had the experience. Was it, as conventional science believed, purely a matter of brain? Or was it a process of consciousness? As an expert in brain function, he was aware of a paradox. Over 60 per cent of NDEs in his sample began when the patient was unconscious. And yet, according to conventional science, an unconscious person cannot use their brain to create or map a 'cognitive model' (an internal or external experience). Similarly, it was believed, memory does not function during unconsciousness. So, if unconscious people and those who had

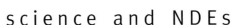

'The true mystery of the world is the visible, not the invisible.'

Oscar Wilde

been certified dead were having cohesive experiences of which they retained a vivid memory, it did not accord with conventional understanding of the brain.

Right-brain experience

In some of Fenwick's cases, not only were the people unconscious, or outwardly dead, but their brain had been severely damaged and so, according to the conventional view, they could not have been experiencing anything. And yet their reports were remarkably close to those of people who did not have brain damage.

If the brain was the cause, rather than the recorder, of an NDE, everything pointed to right-brain involvement. Strong emotions and images are usually present in an NDE, as are feelings of absolute reality, unity and 'knowingness'. Sense of time is lost, déjà vu occurs and intuition is heightened. Beautiful music is often heard. All of these are functions of the right brain. Peter Fenwick reached the conclusion that, while there must be brain structures that mediate NDEs, mystical experiences and the like, at the same time there was a transpersonal element to the experience that depended on mind rather than being inextricably linked to brain. Science is, of course, still arguing the brain versus mind or consciousness paradox – although it comes down heavily on the side of the brain-producing-mind theory. People who have had an NDE indisputably *know*. And as Peter Fenwick points out:

'If we have never personally had such an experience, we can only theorize. And while theories are fine, and fun and even useful, I believe that we can learn more about its true significance by listening to the people who have been there, who have had first-hand experience of what the rest of us can only talk about.'

a stranger in paradise

Julie Chimes was severely attacked by a paranoid schizophrenic.
At the point of death several times, somehow she eventually managed
to escape and pulled through.

In doing so, Julie opened up an intuitive connection that now under-pins her life's work. This is an extraordinary story, the more remarkable for the degree of forgiveness Julie brought to the whole experience. Having been stabbed repeatedly, weak from loss of blood, she suddenly moved out of searing pain and everything became still:

'I was on a trapeze, swinging among the most brilliant stars I had ever seen, suspended in a vast, black-velvet night sky, I rocketed back and forth, through the heavens. The speed exhilarating – the vision intoxicating – my entire being exploding with the excitement of its new-found freedom, beyond the strait-jacket rigidity of its earthly overcoat. There was no sound except the rhythmic beating of a heart. Time did not exist. Nothing mattered. I knew some tiny part of me was being stabbed, and it did not seem to be of any consequence … I was so incredibly alive … I became aware of thoughts, calm, loving, soothing, beautiful thoughts.'

She could distinctly see the frenzied

attack, and yet Julie felt a sense of oneness with her assailant. Knowing with certainty that she would not die, Julie looked directly into her attacker's eyes and said: 'I love you.' She felt an overwhelming sense of love and compassion for this woman who had inflicted such harm.

Julie's perception of the world changed in that moment. She was linked to every conversation and each thought taking place. She found that, if she concentrated on a thought, she was instantly transported to where it was occurring. She moved out of time – past, present and future were laid out before her. She thought of Christ and immediately found herself kneeling before him at the crucifixion. Feeling utterly desolate, she asked him where he was going and how she would find him when he was gone. He replied: 'Everywhere you look you will see Me.'

'I flew back into the heavens, the screen before me was now filled with a light which shone with a brightness beyond anything I had ever seen. All the images of life blended into a sea of dazzling points of

'I flew back into the heavens, the screen before me was now filled with a light which shone with a brightness beyond anything I had ever seen.'

light … somehow everything was me … I was part of a magnificent whole.'

Julie found herself in a wonderful garden where an orange-robed man was supervising two boys practising martial arts. Although he did not use words, she clearly heard his instruction to watch the class. He was showing the boys how to move slowly and turn the attacker's strength against him. Looking at Julie, he said: 'It is very simple. It will get you out of any situation.'

Returning to reality

Back on earth, with a broken knife slicing at her chest, Julie put the lesson into practice. Instead of struggling, she ducked. Her attacker fell forward, the knife embedded itself in the stairs, and Julie slid away. In danger of collapse, she was surprised to hear someone in her head instructing her to leave the house immediately. Unable to move alone, she was guided by the voice and, once more, told to use the power of her attacker. She allowed herself to be propelled backward to the front door.

Unconscious guidance

When Julie left her body this time, there was no magical place waiting. She assumed she must be dead, but questioned who, in that case, was doing the thinking? She was immediately told to go back to her body. Resisting, she continued to question. She was assured that she would survive and that, despite the desperate condition of her physical body, she would not be crippled. Suddenly she found herself back in her body. Once more she was instructed how to handle her attacker. This time she was told to intercept the knife with her right hand. With an enormous amount of trust, she did so. Eventually she was able to open the front door and stagger down the drive, where she collapsed. Urged on by the voice, she crawled onto the road, pursued by her attacker still wielding the knife. A young man confronted the deranged woman, removed the knife and called an ambulance. Julie's partner, a doctor, arrived. He took her to hospital in a police car.

Veritas

In hospital, Julie received more communications from the voice, or, as she came to call it, Veritas. It guided the process of her recovery and explained it was part of Julie's soul-learning programme. This is Julie's understanding of Veritas from *Stranger In Paradise* (p.302), the account of her extraordinary experience: 'You kept reminding me that You were me. I didn't understand. You promised me I would. And now I think I am beginning to. You are the part of me who remembers.

The part who is not sleeping. The part of me who is all-seeing. The part of me who knows only love. The part of me who could take me beyond my physical and mental limitations. The part of me who would teach me how to sustain the knowledge and encourage me never to stop again on my journey into infinite love. Slowly the state of awareness awakening within me realizes it is the destiny of every particle of consciousness to reveal the One within. And with this comes gratitude. The knowledge that I am ordinary, the heart of me the same as everyone else. And with that knowledge a vision of where the path leads ….'

The path led Julie to teach spiritual development work and her love touches everyone she meets. Years later, she says:

'I realized that 'Veritas', the inner voice of my Highest Truth, was in fact the voice that is within each one of us – ours,

Veritas' and mine, was not an exclusive relationship! Knowing and experiencing the wondrous inspiration and guidance from the place within, I now know that the purpose of human birth is to reveal this part of ourselves. All suffering in humanity occurs when this deeper place is not accessed or known. The quest becomes to learn how to distinguish between the constant clatter of the limited conditioned mind (accompanied by the ego's insatiable need to be right while also taking everything personally) and the Inner Voice. Whatever we choose to call 'it', Higher Self, Soul, Truth, Holy Spirit, Love, Buddha Mind, Chi, Brahman, Allah, God or the term everyone can relate to, Intuition, 'it' awaits each one of us in the place beyond limitation. A journalist once asked, "Your assailant heard voices too and she is classed as schizophrenic – aren't you the same?" It was a good question, a big question. My answer then and now is that the voice of the Self has the qualities of love, compassion, wisdom and strength, and each word is permeated with these expansive qualities, spoken only to uplift, encourage, inspire and unite us. The voice of fear has a very different resonance. Its voice is cunning and can often convince us

'When two hearts open in the name of love, all consciousness rejoices: welcome to paradise.'

Veritas

that it, fear, is our truth, and one way to identify it is that it will always preach separation.

Spiritual awakening

Throughout eternity the saints, sages, mystics and gurus have spoken to us about the mysterious and sacred spiritual awakening and have guided our footsteps on the path heading toward home. Since the moment that dear old carving knife entered my chest my process of awakening began, and until my last breath this life is dedicated to the spiritual journey. We each have our own unique moment of touching the feet of the Divine but some of us need rather dramatic cosmic kicks to shake us free from our delusions! I subsequently discovered that the only way to keep the Inner door open is through meditation – the turning of the senses from without to within. I use the term meditation in the widest sense, for there are many wonderful paths which still the senses, quieten the mind, focus the intention in order to reveal the Ultimate. The flashes of Intuition then become more frequent, steadier and easier to identify – they are the keys which can unlock the gates of Paradise.

The source of intuition

Through writing, 'one to one' counselling, and leading seminars, workshops and discussion groups, I have become a guide for those who are ready and willing to embark upon the greatest adventure available to human consciousness – namely the search for Truth, to know the inner being, to understand the source from whence Intuition arises.'

[Julie Chimes can be contacted on juliechimes@hotmail.com.]

CHAPTER three

Metaphysics

'Intuition lets in the light.'

Steve Nation

the metaphysical world view

In the metaphysical view of the world, everything is interconnected.
Nothing is separate and everything communicates intuitively. It is individual
consciousness that creates an illusion of separateness.

Whether it be the Buddhist concept of mind, Hindu Brahman, Sufi nur, esoteric Spirit or the Web of Life, the shamanic dark sea of awareness, or the notion of pure consciousness, there is a subtle substance that interpenetrates matter and is present in the innermost self and the furthest reaches of the universe. Indeed, it is the universe in all its forms and dimensions.

And it is the human soul – or mind or individual consciousness – which metaphysics, in any case, considers to be an illusion of separateness.

In metaphysics, there is no division between individual awareness and universal consciousness. It is as though there is a universal neural net linking each and every part. It is through this interconnection, or consciousness, that intuition functions.

'One's soul is a reverberation of the universe.'

Oscar Kokoschka, *On the Nature of Vision*

'Consciousness creates reality.'
Amit Goswami, *The Self Aware Universe*

'Mind is the universal seed.'
Saraha's *Treasury of Songs*

'Consciousness is the source of all things and of all conceptions. It is a sea ringed about with visions.'
Oscar Kokoschka, *On the Nature of Vision*

'[In the Islamic view] intuition is … revelation through a mysterious faculty different from mind; yet it comes through mindless mind. The knowledge which intuition obtains comes as a result of a mysterious identification of the consciousness with the unseen worlds. These worlds are made up of luminous matter called nur, *existing in sheaths within sheaths,* nurun ala nur. *Man is connected with all these worlds.'*
M.H. Abdi

In metaphysics, our five everyday senses create an illusion of separateness and the perception of the world as we know it. However, there is an energy field which unites the whole and which is visible to the trained eye.

'The sorcerers of ancient Mexico saw that the universe at large is composed of energy fields in the form of luminous filaments. They saw zillions of them … They also saw those energy fields arrange themselves into currents of luminous fibers, streams that are constant, perennial forces in the universe … These energy fields are converted into sensory data, and the sensory data is then interpreted and perceived as the world we know … What turns the luminous fibers into sensory data is the dark sea of awareness.'
Carlos Castaneda, *The Active Side of Infinity*

'The solidity of the material world has proved illusory: it can be resolved into particles and energy. In certain circumstances the particles themselves dissolve into energy of radiation, and this label proclaims our inability to say any more. We only think the material world is solid and coloured and extensive in space and time because of the sort of special senses and minds which we possess. These select for us the qualities of the world we know.'
Raynor C. Johnson, *The Imprisoned Splendour*

Mystics of all ages and persuasions have penetrated the illusion of separateness and moved into wholeness. Poets eloquently express this experience, as these moving extracts show:

'In the higher realms of true Suchness
There is neither self nor other
When direct identification is sought
We can only say, Not two.
One in All,
All in One.
The Heart Sutra

When you touch the place that T.S. Eliot described as 'the intersection of the timeless with time', you reach the source of intuition.

*One instant I, an instant knew
As God knows it. And it and you
I, above Time, oh, blind! Could see
In witless immortality.'*
Rupert Brooke, *Dining Room Tea*

*'Gone is the sense of a separate, finite
self, with its individual gains and
losses, its personal hopes and fears, and
in its place comes the experience of the
One Atman, abiding in all beings, of
all beings as eddies in that all-pervading
ocean of bliss.'*
Sri Krishna Prem

*'There are in His universe no fences
between the 'natural' and 'supernatural'
worlds; everything is a part of the creative
Play of God, and therefore – even in its
humblest details– capable of revealing
the Player's mind.'*
Evelyn Underhill, *Poems of Kabir*

To be intuitive you do not need to be a mystic or believe in God, the divine, or universal energy, but as you develop your intuition the more you will be aware that there is such an energy. Intuition almost inevitably leads to spiritual awareness and intuition is a by-product of spiritual development. As the Sufi poet Rumi said:

*'Like a mirror my soul displays secrets;
I am able not to speak, but I am unable
not to know.'*

For Rumi, the only worthwhile journey was the inward one into the greater self:

*'And you … choose to journey into
yourself, like a ruby-mine be receptive to a
print from the sunbeams.
Make a journey out of self into self …
for by such a journey earth became a
mine of gold.'*

The more attuned you can become to the greater reality, the more connections you open to pure consciousness or the divine, the greater awareness you will have

of the web of life that connects and interpenetrates everything. The physicist David Bohm had a mystic's eye when he said 'matter is frozen light'.

A dream of reality

Many of the eastern philosophies, such as the Hindu Vedas that predate the Vedanta, assert that creation is a divine dream. The poet Keats reflects Christianity's view when he asserts that we are part of 'God's long immortal dream'. Author Michael Talbot quotes the Kalahari bushmen who say: 'The dream is dreaming itself.' And he points out that it does not matter who is dreaming, it is all part of the whole and states that 'the universe is sustained by an act of such stupendous and ineffable creativity that it simply cannot be reduced to such terms'.

Sri Aurobindo, a mystic by profession, paraphrased the 19th-century mystic and theosophist Madame Blavatsky when he suggested that:

'If you are embarrassed by the word "spirit" think of spirit as the subtlest form of matter. But, if you are not embarrassed by the word spirit, you can think of matter as the densest form of spirit.'

Intuition is spirit. It is consciousness. When you touch the place that T.S. Eliot described as 'the intersection of the timeless with time', you reach the ultimate source of intuition – the place where intuition dwells and spills its wisdom into awareness for those who are able to hear it.

Consciousness

Neuroscientists debate endlessly about consciousness and mind. Most see it as a function or by-product of the brain. Professor Susan Greenfield of Oxford University sums up the scientific viewpoint when she says: 'Consciousness gives purpose to our existence. It is an inner world that meshes with the external one but is always distinct.' For her,

Today I am the North wind on the wing
And the wide roaring of the clamorous sea
And the huge heaven's calm immensity.'

(Rumi, trans. Sir Cecil Spring-Rice)

consciousness is the product of 'transient assemblies of different populations of neurons' in the brain and depends on different arousal states.

Professor Charles Honorton summed up the essential dilemma, asking whether mind 'emerges' out of or represents some 'inner' dimension of physical states or whether mind is an independent entity that interacts with but is not reducible to physical states.

Metaphysicians, however, know consciousness and mind in a much wider form. To them consciousness is immanent within the universe, it is never distinct. Multi-dimensional and cohesive, consciousness is summed up by James Herbert in his novel *Others*:

'The cosmos consists more of energy and consciousness than it does of physical matter … Consciousness is the thing between atoms and molecules and particles, the unseen glue that holds everything together … it's consciousness, which is energy, that binds the patterns and forms shapes, matter.'

Beyond time

If consciousness is one, and separateness is an illusion, there is no barrier to intuition concerning 'another person'. Intuition tunes into that part of consciousness which is manifesting through a different physical body and reads its energy vibrations. What is interesting, however, is that to do this, intuition moves out of time. It goes beyond the illusion of past, present and future into the eternal now. All metaphysicians instinctively by-pass time – and, indeed, space. The exact mechanics may remain a mystery, but once you are able to move outside time and space, the reality of that experience will convince you of its validity.

Moving out of time

Essentially, in our somewhat limited state of everyday awareness, we live on a time line that goes from the past through the present and on to the future. The time line is what we use to make sense of our experiences here on earth. Step off that line, and you move into timelessness, the eternal now.

EXERCISE
Walking the time line

- Draw a chalk line on the floor.
- Stand in the middle of the line in the 'present' position.
- Look 'back' behind you to the past. Walk into it and notice what images come to you and any sensations you may feel.
- Look 'forward' in front of you to the future. Walk into it and notice what images come to you and any sensations

you may feel.
- Close your eyes and step off the line into timelessness.
- How does it feel?

You have the option to step back on the line or choose to live in the eternal now.

the biomagnetic field

*Metaphysically speaking, intuition works in conjunction with
the biomagnetic field that forms a subtle energy shield around the
physical body, sometimes called the aura.*

Visible to intuitives as a shifting, interweaving field of coloured light, the biomagnetic field can be captured by a kirlian camera. Disturbances in it reflect dis-ease that may be physical, emotional, mental or spiritual in origin. Conversely, physical, emotional and mental symptoms may reflect imbalances in the biomagnetic field. Biomagnetic fields are extremely sensitive, and can intermingle with other people's energy fields. When this happens, you unconsciously read from that biomagnetic field and will pick up any energetic disturbances within it. Disturbances in the biomagnetic field may reveal physical diseases, and you could easily pick up a headache from someone with whom your biomagnetic field has intermingled. If the disturbance is emotional, it will be revealed

Disturbances in the biomagnetic field may reveal physical diseases.

through the emotional level of the biomagnetic field. You pick up if someone is happy or depressed through contact with their emotional biomagnetic field. The mental biomagnetic field holds thought impressions and ingrained patterns.

It is possible, but not desirable, for someone else to draw energy from your biomagnetic field, which leaves you feeling depleted; or for you to drain energy from them, which will leave you feeling exhilarated and them exhausted. Getting into the habit of monitoring your biomagnetic field not only protects you, but it also opens you to unconscious intuitions you may have been receiving.

Seeing the biomagnetic field is an intuitive skill that many people have without knowing it. If you tell someone they are looking a little down today, you are probably unconsciously reading their biomagnetic field. If you instinctively avoid someone, you will have seen something unpleasant in their biomagnetic field. Troubled biomagnetic fields look 'down' or 'dark'. Illness shows up as a murky patch over the part of the body affected. You may have caught glimpses of someone's biomagnetic field as a halo of white or coloured light. You can learn to consciously 'see' the biomagnetic field.

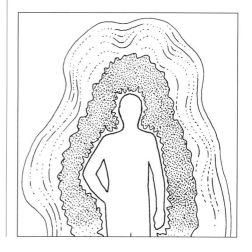

seeing the biomagnetic field

*Paradoxically, you see a biomagnetic field when you are not really
looking. When you first start, it is easiest to see it against a white background
in reasonable but not too bright light.*

EXERCISE

Viewing the field

- Ask the person whose biomagnetic
  field you wish to see to stand against
  a suitable background.
- Letting your eyes half close and go
  out of focus and, looking out of the
  corner of your eye, allow your eyes to
  drift slightly to the side of the person
  and around their head. (If you blink
  and try to focus, the images fades.)
- You will perceive a light fanning out
  around the body.
- With practice you will see the colours
  extending out from the body.

monitoring the biomagnetic field

*Monitoring your biomagnetic field helps you to protect your
energy reserves and ensures that you will not leak precious energy or allow
subtle intrusion into your energy body.*

The following exercise can be performed sitting if you prefer, and with your eyes open or closed.

EXERCISE
Feeling the field

- Stand so that you can reach out around yourself. Take your attention down to the palms of your hands. Put your palms in front of you, facing your body, about a hands' breadth away. Move your hands backward and forward, using your palms to sense where your biomagnetic field is – it may feel tingly or springy.
- Move your hands around the edges of your biomagnetic field from your head to your feet. Begin in front of your body and go from above the head down to your feet. Then do the sides and finally the back of your body. (If you cannot reach with your hands, use your mind to check out this area). Check how far out the biomagnetic field extends and notice any places where the energy breaks up or feels different in any way.
- If you find that your biomagnetic field extends a long way out, or is very close to your body, try moving your biomagnetic field. Use your hand to pull or push it into a more appropriate

distance from your body – well within arm's length and probably closer, depending on the situation.

- Go over your entire biomagnetic field checking for breaks and 'holes' or cold spots. Use your hands to put extra energy into that place, pulling the edges of the biomagnetic field together. You can picture healing light sealing it together.

- Experiment with the ability your mind has to control your biomagnetic field. Close your eyes. Picture your biomagnetic field expanding and contracting. Really let yourself feel the process happening. Push it in and draw it out until you feel competent. Let your biomagnetic field settle at an appropriate distance from your body.

- When you are ready, open your eyes. Take your attention down to your feet and feel your feet on the earth. Be aware that your feet are connected to the earth, grounding you. Take your attention to your forehead and picture a shield closing like that over an automatic camera lens. With your eyes wide open, take a deep breath and stand up with your feet firmly on the earth.

'A moment's insight is sometimes worth a life's experiences.'

Oliver Wendell Holmes

expanding your awareness

Once you have mastered the art of monitoring your own
biomagnetic field, you can expand this ability so that you become aware
of the field of any living being or substance.

Practise the monitoring exercise once or twice a day until you can sense your biomagnetic field by mentally scanning your body. You will know instinctively if your energy starts to drain or if something tries to invade your biomagnetic field, and will automatically seal it. (If you find it difficult to visualize, you can use a clear quartz or selenite crystal to work over the biomagnetic field, healing and sealing it.)

Developing your sensitivity

When you have mastered the art of monitoring your own biomagnetic field, ask a friend to allow you to feel their biomagnetic field. Impart to them any impressions you receive as you move your hands over their body about a hand's breath out from their clothes – some people find it easier to do this using a crystal as an intermediary. Be sure to notice 'cold' or 'hot spots', areas where the biomagnetic field extends outward, places where the biomagnetic field feels weak, and whether your own body picks up any sensations, particularly pain. Try to sense whether this is happening at a physical, emotional or mental level – you can pick up clues about this by noticing how far away from the body your hand is. Close is in the physical level, next layer out is the emotional level, and then the mental level. You can also take note of what is happening in your own solar plexus at the time. It may react dramatically.

Try this energetic sensing on your pets. Many pets respond well and if you hold your hand on a place where you feel a lack of energy, you can picture light entering the spot and re-energizing it. Your hand will tell you when the weakened area has been rebalanced.

Food and energy

Energy sensing is an extremely useful skill for checking on the freshness of food and whether it still has energy. Some food has been over-processed or hangs around for so long that it loses its life force. Bioenergetic sensing warns you when this has happened.

You can use your sensing ability to check out crystals to see if they have a clear energy or if they need cleaning. You can also check whether objects or substances will be good for you or detrimental to your health and well-being.

Cleansing your biomagnetic field is a useful daily habit to form. It only takes a few moments before you sleep and ensures nothing detrimental is carried over to the next day.

If you are kinaesthetic, you may prefer to do your biomagnetic field cleansing with a crystal. Smoky quartz, amethyst and clear quartz are all excellent for this. After you have finished, remember to clean your crystal by holding it under running water for a few moments and leaving it in the sun to re-energize.

EXERCISE
Cleaning the magnetic field

Picture a hand-held vacuum cleaner, the kind you use to clean out the car. Picture yourself running this vacuum cleaner over the whole of your biomagnetic field, hoovering up anything that is sticking to it. Make sure you do the back as well as the front. When you have finished, take the dust bag out of the hoover. Picture a shiny new dustbin ready to receive the dust and dirt. It will be emptied by the cosmic trash man. When you have emptied the bag, replace it into the vacuum ready for use next time.

When you are ready, open your eyes. Take your attention down to your feet and feel your feet on the earth. Be aware that your feet are connected to the earth, grounding you. Take your attention to your forehead and picture a shield closing over your third eye. With your eyes wide open, take a deep breath and stand up with your feet firmly on the earth.

EXERCISE
Using a crystal

Hold the crystal in your hand and slowly 'comb' all over your biomagnetic field, about a hand's breadth out from your body.

the chakras

The chakras connect your biomagnetic field and your physical body (see the illustration opposite) and act, among other things, as linkage points to higher consciousness and spiritual energies.

If a chakra is either blocked or is stuck open it can affect your energy field, leaving you vulnerable to outside influences. Certain of your chakras need to be open if you are using your intuition (experience will indicate which).

Earth Chakra *(below the feet)*

This chakra grounds you in your body and in the physical world. When this chakra is permanently closed, it is difficult to operate in everyday reality. If it is permanently open, you can easily pick up negative energies from the ground, which may contaminate your intuition.

Base *(bottom of the spine)* and Sacral Chakras *(below the navel)*

These are the sexual and creative chakras. They can be the site of 'emotional hooks' which drain your energy. You are vulnerable here to another person through sexual contact or powerful feelings such as lust or possessiveness. If you keep the base chakra open when using your intuition, it helps you to ground it into everyday reality.

Solar Plexus Chakra *(between waist and heart)*

This chakra is an emotional linkage point.

This is where you store your emotional baggage, and where you keep the buttons that reactivate it. This baggage is out of sight in your subconscious mind but the colours of those emotions will show in both the chakra and the biomagnetic body associated with it. Intuition can easily be contaminated by your own emotional baggage or that of someone else, especially as another person may, either knowingly or unknowingly, press one of these buttons and bring about a reaction that is out of all proportion to the event.

Invasion and energy leeching also take place through this chakra. A solar plexus chakra that is 'stuck open' means you take on other people's feelings easily, but if you can learn to open and close the chakra at will, you will be able to read other people's emotions and yet remain detached. You may well begin to receive

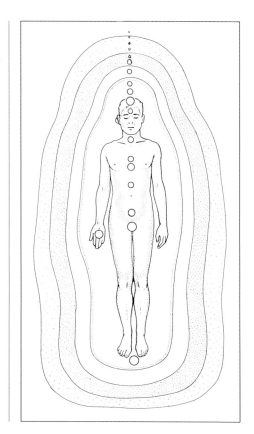

intuitions through your solar plexus as you unconsciously read other people's emotions quite clearly.

Heart Chakra *(in the centre of the chest)*

The heart chakra is another emotional and relationship linkage point. It is the seat of love in all its manifestations. An open and fully functioning heart chakra is essential for metaphysical health. Many people find that their intuition functions best when their heart is expanded. Sending love to someone from your heart naturally attunes you to their energies and helps you to communicate more effectively.

Higher Heart *(above the heart)*

This is the chakra of unconditional love and a spiritual connector. It can act as a protector for the heart and a powerful contact point for intuitive guidance.

Throat and Brow Chakras
(third eye)

These chakras work at mental and intuitive levels and are involved in communicating intuition. Strong beliefs can block these chakras. A blocked throat chakra results in difficulty in communication – especially not being able to speak your truth. Problems can arise from your own unvoiced intuitions. If the third eye or brow chakra is stuck open, you are vulnerable to the thoughts, feelings and influences not only of people around you on the earth level, but also on the etheric level. You may feel constantly bombarded with thoughts and feelings that are not your own. You may also receive indiscriminate 'psychic messages' and not be able to filter these out. You may be prey to premonitions of doom, wild intuitions and the like – not all of which will come from outside yourself.

Inner ear (*behind the ear*)

These chakras connect to your inner voice and to clairaudience. If stuck open, Ménière's disease can result, as can harassment by etheric voices or sensitivity to noise.

Crown Chakra (*top of the head*) and Higher Crown Chakras (*above the head*)

The chakras connect to the spiritual level and to higher consciousness. People with these chakras stuck open will be ungrounded and may be unable to earth high spiritual connections. Intuition can pour down through these chakras, as can channelled information. If these chakras are not under your conscious control, or if only the first one or two higher crown chakras are open, you may connect with beings in the etheric realms who do not have the best of intentions. Such beings can be misleading and malicious and intuitions received via this source are extremely unreliable, even though they may masquerade as the highest possible guidance.

The ideal situation is for all the chakras to be balanced, opening and closing at will, under your conscious control by the power of thought.

protecting your chakras

Protecting and being in control of your chakras opening are both useful tools in developing your intuition, as you can filter psychic input or environmental factors when necessary.

EXERCISE
Chakra shields

- Sitting comfortably in an upright chair, close your eyes and establish a gentle breathing rhythm.
- Take your attention down to your feet and the point between and slightly below them. If this chakra is open, you will be aware of your connection with the earth and you may feel energy from the earth travelling up from this chakra through your feet. If this chakra is stuck, you may feel ungrounded and 'floaty'. Picture a pair of gates shutting off this chakra between it and the earth beneath it. Then let them open again. Picture the gates opening and closing until they come under your conscious control.
- Now move your attention up to the base of your spine. Visualize a whirling vortex of energy and picture a pair of shields closing over the spot, shutting out the light (use your hands if this helps). Practise opening and closing these shields a few times until it becomes automatic. (You will be able to sense the difference within your body as the chakra opens and closes.)
- Bring your attention to the sacral

chakra below your navel. Picture this full of light, and close the shields across. Open and close this chakra until it is automatic.

- Bring your attention up to your solar plexus, again visualize the chakra open, and then close it off with shields.

- Move up to the heart chakra, opening and closing it a few times. (You may also be able to sense the higher heart chakra, in which case practise opening and closing this.)

- Now take your attention to your throat chakra. Open and close it before moving up to open and close the third-eye brow chakra, and finally move to the top of your head for the crown and higher crown chakras.

- Once you can open and close the chakras at will, practise running your mind up and down your spine to assess the state of your chakras. Before you bring your attention back into the room, take your mind to your earth chakra.

- Check whether this is open or closed and sense if you are in an area of environmental or geopathic stress. Open or close your earth chakra as appropriate according to the energies of the place where you are, and check that your third eye is also closed.

- Bring your attention fully back into the room. Stand up and feel your feet firmly on the floor. Have a good stretch and breathe deeply to ground yourself.

- If you are kinaesthetic, you can use your hands to 'read' your chakras and to open and close them. Once you have programmed in the opening and closing by moving your hands, it will become an automatic action carried out by your mind.

chakra cleansing

Chakras can hold on to negative energies or emotions. Cleansing the chakras is essential for healthy functioning and maximum protection, and to avoid contaminating intuition.

You can clean the chakras with the power of the mind alone, using visualization, or by creating a simple but extremely powerful crystal layout.

EXERCISE
Cleansing with visualization

• Repeat the exercise on pages 92–93, this time checking out the colour and spin of each chakra in turn. If the chakra looks murky or has dark patches, visualize light entering the chakra to cleanse it. If it is spinning too fast or too slow, use the power of your mind to set it to the right speed – you will know intuitively when it is right.

• See the light whirling round until all the blackness is cleared. When you have finished, all the chakras should have an equal brightness and energy intensity (do not worry if some seem to spin in different directions).

• Complete the exercise by opening the earth chakra (as long as the environmental energies are clean) and closing the chakras along the spine and head. Bring your attention fully back into the room. Feel your feet contacting the floor and be aware of your connection with the earth. Breathe deeply and have a good stretch to remind yourself that you are fully present in your body.

Crystal cleansing

Chakra cleansing can also be carried out with crystals. By selecting appropriate crystals, you can clean, re-energize and harmonize the energy centres. Lie down for approximately 20 minutes with appropriate crystals placed on each chakra. Start at your feet with a brown crystal and work up your body using red and orange at the base and sacral, yellow for the solar plexus, green for the heart, blue-green for the higher heart, blue for the throat, indigo for the third eye, purple for the crown and clear or light amethyst for the higher crown chakras. Otherwise, use the special crystals indicated opposite.

CRYSTALS FOR THE CHAKRAS

higher crown • selenite
crown • clear quartz
brow/third eye • lapis lazuli
throat • turquoise
higher heart • kunzite
heart • rose quartz
solar plexus • malachite
sacral • carnelian
base • bloodstone
earth • smoky quartz

CHAPTER four

The science of intuition

'Major scientific progress has always occurred when the leading paradigm has seriously failed to account for some significant findings ... if instead of rejecting and ridiculing new observations, we would consider them an exciting opportunity and conduct

our own study to test them,
we might very likely find that the
reports were accurate.
When that happens, we will realize
that the nature of human beings is
very different from what is being
taught at Western universities.'

Professor Stanislav Grof, *Thinking Beyond the Brain*

science and intuition

In the 150 years that scientists have been studying psi, they have proved to their own satisfaction many of the things that intuition is not but have thrown very little light on what it actually is, or the mechanism by which it functions.

Scientists have now ruled out most of the presently known subtle energies such as electromagnetism, but the search continues to find an explanation of how intuition works. Quantum physics seems to offer a glimpse of possibilities but it is a highly complex field and, as one eminent scientist said, 'If you think you understand quantum, you don't.' It is the meeting point of science, consciousness and mysticism.

A unified field

Religion and metaphysics have long postulated the existence of a spiritually unifying force: Mind, God, Great Spirit, Brahman and so on. As the *Mundaka Upanishad* put it 3,000 years ago:

> 'Everything that sways, breathes,
> opens, closes, lives in Spirit; beyond
> learning, beyond everything, better than
> anything; living, unliving.'
> (trans. William Butler Yeats and
> Shree Purohit Swami)

Science is now supporting this unifying force with exciting discoveries in quantum physics and the development of a unified field theory.

Quantum physicist Werner Heisenberg has declared that 'the idea that living things are chemistry and physics with no living force contradicts quantum theory' and in *Wholeness and the Implicate Order*, the physicist David Bohm theorizes that we are actually unified by space, arguing that a dynamic, flowing wholeness underlying the parts is a greater reality than the apparently separate parts: 'Each relatively autonomous and stable structure (e.g. an atomic particle) is to be understood not as something independently and permanently existent but rather as a product that has been formed in the whole flowing movement and that will ultimately dissolve back into this movement.' An insight that was known to the writer of the ancient *Mundaka Upanishad*: 'The sparks, though of one nature with the fire, leap from it, uncounted beings leap from the Everlasting, but these, my son, merge into It again. The Everlasting is shapeless, birthless, breathless, mindless, above everything, outside everything, inside everything.' A description that sounds exactly like the universe from the perspective of a quantum physicist.

LEVEL	VEDANTA	BURCKHARDT HEIM	NUMBER OF DIMENSIONS
4	Divine	Aeonic	6
3	Causal	Entelechy	5
2	Subtle	Time	2
1	Gross	Space	3

QUANTUM FACTORS

- In the physics of the fundamental particles that make up an atom, some are considered to have zero mass except when moving. Of all the particles that make up our bodies, there are 10 to the 9, i.e. 1000,000,000 more particles with zero mass than there are particles that have mass. From this scientific view, only one thousandth millionth part is matter. The rest is energy. Quantum physics sees photons as controlling matter and photons have zero mass. In other words, energy controls matter and psi is an energy.
- Fundamental particles such as electrons, protons, neutrons, photons and neutrinos can influence each other at a considerable distance, a concept known as non-locality.
- '[Everything is] interconnected in such a way that the properties of the smallest pieces depend on the properties of the whole.' (Fritjof Capra)
- Quantum theory postulates the existence of particles that apparently move backward in time.
- 'In some strange sense the quantum principle tells us that we are dealing with a participatory universe.' (Professor John Wheeler, *The Universe as Home for Man*)
- One quantum particle can be in two places at once.
- Quantum particles come into existence when observed.

Quantum intuition

The holy grail of physics has been to find a unified field theory that can explain the action of gravitational forces, electro-magnetism and the strong and weak intra-nuclear forces that bind atoms together. Existing theories, like the theory of relativity, could explain some, but not all, of how these forces will act, why they exist and similar questions.

The Quantum Field Theory put forward by Burckhardt Heim can explain the four forces, and computer predictions made using the theory seem to predict accurately physical and observed phenomena – which suggests that the theory may be correct. The theory postulates a universe on four levels and having six dimensions rather than the previously scientifically accepted four. The ancient Vendantic system also suggested that there were four multi-dimensional levels roughly equating to Heim's levels, Vedanta being a 3,000-year-old science of consciousness. Heim's theory, in tandem with Vedanta, also puts forward the idea that the control mechanisms of living organisms exist at the level of the fifth dimension and are therefore outside four-dimensional space and time.

Across time and space

If our control mechanisms exist outside time and space, you would expect that it would be possible to intuit the future, revisit the past, know what is happening at a distance or communicate with beings who are outside four-dimensional time and space. However, quantum physics goes further than this in suggesting that quantum particles can inhabit any or none of these levels simultaneously, thus transferring information patterns over great distances and, apparently, time. This explains phenomena like precognition, telepathy and remote viewing.

Riding the crest of a wave

Quantum physics suggests energy is not continuous but rather exists as packs of energy – energy that behaves like particles and yet can act like a wave. In discussing consciousness and quantum physics with Jeffrey Mishlove back in 1987, theoretical quantum physicist Dr Fred Alan Wolf suggested that 'consciousness is a huge oceanic wave that washes through everything, and it has ripples and vibrations in it. When there are acts of consciousness, the wave turns into bubbles at that moment, it turns to froth'. He pointed out that everything, human beings included, is composed of this froth and that is how we would see ourselves under an electron microscope: 'A rather bizarre-looking light show, of things popping on and off, vanishing and reappearing, matter created out of nothing and then vanishing. And in that vanishing and creation, an electromagnetic signal is piped from one point to another point.'

Dr Wolf also pointed out that quantum physics gives 'a real mathematical basis for saying actions in the future can have an

'Envision yourself out there in the future with something about yourself better than it is now.'

Dr Fred Alan Wolf

effect on the probability patterns that exist in the present'. In other words, it is possible that insights that you are having in 20 years' time are actually reaching back to have an effect on your present. To make absolutely sure that this happens, Dr Wolf suggested envisioning yourself out there in the future with something about yourself better than it is now. That vision would propagate back to the present, affecting the choices you make now so that what you envision would come to pass. This means that quantum physics supports the validity of positive thinking and visualization.

The holographic universe

Vedantic philosophy sees the world as *maya* or illusion, a projection. Strangely enough, this ancient esoteric concept is being mirrored by pioneering scientists who believe that the universe is a giant, three-dimensional holographic illusion – what author Michael Talbot describes as 'ghostly images, projections from a level of reality so far beyond our own that it is literally beyond both space and time'. (A hologram is a system where a part contains the information of the whole.)

This idea was independently arrived at by David Bohm, a quantum physicist from London University, and Karl Pribram, a neurophysiologist from Stanford University. Bohm reached his conclusions when seeking an overall 'umbrella' for all the various phenomena encountered in quantum physics, whereas Pribram turned to a hologram to resolve the problems he encountered in trying to explain the workings of the brain and such things as memory and perception. Both men, however, quickly realized that the holographic model not only solved their particular puzzles, but could also account for previously inexplicable phenomena such as synchronicity, psychic abilities, intuition and mystical experiences.

The controversial theory has been in existence for a comparatively short time, just over 30 years, but it was almost immediately embraced by doctors and scientists at the leading edge of psychical investigation, and supported by research such as that by Alain Aspect of the French Institute of Theoretical and Applied Optics, who demonstrated that the subatomic particles that comprise the physical universe – the fabric of our reality – are holographic in nature.

Underpinning the model is the theory that brains are also holographic in nature. Pribram, after extensive investigation into brain function, especially in the areas of memory and vision, came to see that 'the wave-front nature of brain-cell connectivity' created by electrical activity in the brain was an 'endless and kaleidoscopic array' of patterns which created a hologram with an enormous capacity for information storage and the ability to create reality. Pribram's discoveries led him to consider whether what mystics throughout the ages had been saying was true – that the world is an illusion. Seeking the answer led him to David Bohm.

A conscious universe

In Bohm's view, the universe itself is a hologram. The chameleon-like ability of subatomic phenomena such as electrons to be either particles or waves and the mysterious interconnections that occurred between seemingly unrelated subatomic events were paradoxes that needed a new view of the world. Bohm conceived the revolutionary notion that the parts were actually organized by the quantum whole and had the property of non-locality – that is, they did not exist in time and space. Information contained within a hologram is non-local.

In a hologram, one tiny fragment or numerous tiny fragments contain the image of the whole but the image is not visible to the naked eye. It is hidden or unfolded within the hologram until it is projected out to the world. This led Bohm to believe that there are two kinds of order, the enfolded or implicate order, a deep, indivisible level of reality which underlies apparent reality; and the explicate or unfolded order which is everyday reality. He envisioned a flowing movement between the implicate and explicate order, preferring the name holomovement to hologram as this was less static.

According to Bohm, consciousness is a subtle form of matter that is present in both the implicate and explicate order. His idea that everything, animate or inanimate, in the universe is alive and is consciousness resonates with the ancient Vedantic notion of Brahman emanating throughout creation.

The holographic model of the universe, especially the notion that consciousness is an integral part of it, allows intuition and abilities such as moving out of time and space to flourish. In a hologram any part of the whole can be accessed by shining a laser through it at any point. Steve Nation's assertion that 'intuition lets in the light' could one day be supported by science.

CHAPTER five

Developing intuition

'When you let intuition have its way with you, you open up new levels of the world. Such opening-up is the most practical of all activities.'

Evelyn Underhill

your intuition

In this section you will find a series of carefully structured introductory exercises to expand and focus your intuitive awareness and develop your extrasensory perception.

The exercises will help you to expand your individual awareness and access wider consciousness. They should be worked through in order and built upon until you feel totally confident you are ready to move on to the next stage. Do not rush and do not skip anything because something else looks more exciting. You need to do the groundwork first so that you are in control of the process. This will make you all the more competent when it is time to explore other realms.

The best tools you can develop alongside your intuition are common sense and discernment. While some experiences will make you go 'Whaaat?!' and yet still be valuable, others may well be internal sabotage or external trickery. Questioning your experiences, rather than blindly accepting everything, will make your intuition that much more valuable.

You can either read the exercises first and memorize them, or tape them, with pauses when necessary, and play them to yourself. You can introduce appropriate music into the background.

Appraising your intuitive function
It is important that you do the next

exercise before you read any further in the book. It will help you to recognize how your intuitive faculties work. Ask a friend to assist you with this and to observe you carefully as you do it. It would be useful if your friend read the questions overleaf first and made notes as you do the exercise. (If you cannot ask anyone to assist, try to be aware of how your body and mind are behaving as you do the exercise, or make a video or computer movie of yourself giving the directions.)

• Give your friend directions from your house, or place of work, to the nearest supermarket. (You can give directions for either walking or taking some form of transport. If you find it impossible, a map is printed opposite for you to use.)

• Be as specific as you can. When you have finished, answer the questions in consultation with your friend.

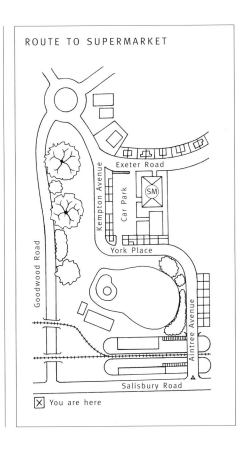

ROUTE TO SUPERMARKET

Exeter Road
Kempton Avenue
Car Park
SM
York Place
Goodwood Road
Aintree Avenue
Salisbury Road
X You are here

- Did your eyelids flutter as you gave directions?
- In which direction did your eyes point?
- Were your eyes closed or open?
- Did you see a mental picture of the route?
- Did you use your hands?
- Did you draw a map?
- Did your body move?
- Did you hear a voice giving directions?
- Did you 'just know' the way?
- Did you find it difficult to verbalize?
- Did you have difficulty distinguishing between left and right?

Assessing the result

When giving directions almost everyone visualizes, although you may not be aware that you are doing this. Eyelids fluttering rapidly – as they do when you dream – are an indication that you are indeed visualizing. If your eyes move around, you are accessing different parts of your brain.

If your eyes are up above the horizontal, you are using the visual cortex. If you close your eyes in order to see better, and especially if you saw a mental map, you are working at a visual level and your intuition will function visually.

Kinaesthetics

If you drew a map, used your hands to indicate direction, or moved your body around, you are kinaesthetic. Your intuition works through your body and through feeling. You will be prone to hunches and gut feelings.

Aural

If you heard an inner voice giving you directions which you passed on, your intuition functions aurally. You may well have supersensitive hearing, and are easily disturbed by noise (in which case, you may find that playing music as you do the exercises in this book actually interferes with your intuition).

Sensing and feeling

If you stood there and gave directions without moving, seeing or hearing anything because you 'just knew' them, you may well find that you already function on a sensing or feeling level. If you found you confused left and right – and especially if you did not realize that you were doing so – you are most probably right-brain dominant and will find imagery easy to access but verbalizing more difficult.

You can also establish whether you are a visual person or an aural one by trying to remember a telephone number you don't know off by heart. Do you see it written down in front of you? Do you make writing motions as you try to remember? Or do you hear the person saying the number? If it's the former, you are visual. If it's the latter, you are aural. If you make writing motions, you are kinaesthetic. Some people combine two or three. If you are an aural person, orientated toward hearing rather than seeing, you may find it easier to drop your eyes slightly rather than raising them. If you focus on the area to the back of your ears, you may well begin to hear your intuition communicating with you. You may have to adapt the guided visualizations slightly. You could concentrate on the sounds and smells of your favourite place, for instance, hearing bird song or the sound of the sea.

keeping an intuition journal

*Keeping an Intuition Journal regularly is vital if you are to gain
full benefit from this book and learn to access your intuition in the most
efficient and appropriate way possible.*

You can develop this intuitive facility by keeping your Intuition Journal. Select a large book that you keep specially for the purpose. Write in the present tense: 'I am seeing …' 'There is …' As you write, you may find yourself recalling something that happened in a meditation or exercise but which you did not consciously remember. Or you may find that new information comes. Let it.

Always date each entry and give an indication of time and whether it was an exercise, a dream, an intuitive feeling and so on. (Timing events may pinpoint a period of the day or month when you are more receptive as there are certain parts of the bioenergetic and endocrine cycles that are particularly conducive to ESP.) You can also add any unusual features with regard to mood, weather and so on.

Making connections

If you get into the habit of recording your experiences you will have a useful tool for developing your intuition. It is only when you look back and link up disparate incidents that you can begin to discern patterns and 'wholes'.

Relying on memory is unwise – it is

easy to overlook small details that add up to a big picture. When you begin working metaphysically, information often comes in 'pieces'. You may need several sessions to put them together into a coherent whole.

By recording everything that happens, you also begin to pick up signals. The greater part of intuitive communication occurs at the subliminal level. It is easy to miss the cues. If you write down what you 'saw' or 'heard', paying attention at the same time to how your body feels as you review the experience, you may well pick up details that you did not notice the first time round.

You may get body signals in the form of twitches or jerks, strange facial expressions, and sensations. Record these in your journal. The graphic twitches and jerks that can accompany the opening up of intuition usually indicate that you are a kinaesthetic person. Your body is responding to signals

'A good artist lets their intuition lead them wherever it wants.'

Lao Tzu

that your mind cannot yet make conscious. If you allow the process to happen naturally, you will gradually become conscious of what your body is saying to you and what the signals mean.

Some signals are subtle – for example, it took me weeks to realize that the touch on my shoulder as a meditation session began was actually a gatekeeper saying 'I'm here'. I had been expecting to 'see' a gatekeeper, not feel him. Similarly, a discarnate guide indicated his presence by a prickling on my scalp. That was 30 years ago, and I now take it for granted that they are there when I need them – I do not require signals. They, and other aspects of my intuition, do what I call a 'straight through job'. Words flow out of my fingers as I type, or out of my mouth as I talk. I am often surprised, but never dismayed. Over time, I have learnt to trust my intuition. It is essential to record sessions like this because they seem to bypass the memory cells. Clients often tell me that it was remarkable that I had said such and such on the tape I prepared for them. I have no

Your journal can also be used to note down any random thoughts, impressions, perceptions and good ideas that you have at any time.

memory of having done so. (I could not, in any case, hold on to all the information that passes through me in this way.)

Writing meditation

Writing at random without pause, and without censoring yourself, for five or ten minutes straight after meditation, is another way to develop this ability. However, it is essential that you use your common sense.

Do not immediately act on what it says. Remember that you are still learning and should test out the information. Is it coming from the highest possible source and for your highest good? (Even when you are experienced it is still a good idea to test it out. Do not become complacent – the ego or wishful thinking is quick to slip in.) If you have any doubt, put it aside. Have a mental filing cabinet into which such things go. Periodically, take them out

and see if they fit in with anything else you've received.

Your journal can also be used to note down any random thoughts, impressions, perceptions and good ideas that you have at any time. This is an excellent practice to adopt. Only about 2 per cent of the population keep a journal, but virtually all 'geniuses' are within that percentage. It ensures that you overlook nothing, and reinforces your intuitions.

Reinforcing awareness

Make a note of any action you take about an intuition, whether you understood it completely, and whether it was successful. Carry your journal with you so that you will always be able to record these moments as they occur. The more you keep a record, the more useful thoughts you will receive. Responding to subtle awareness reinforces that awareness.

FARADAY: THE INTUITIVE SCIENTIST

Michael Faraday, the great 19th-century scientist, was never formally educated and could not understand mathematics. Coming from a desperately poor background in Victorian England, he was taught to read and write at a Sunday school and then educated himself by reading the books he bound in his work as an apprentice bookbinder. As a result, he preserved his ability to think inventively and described the process as one of visual insights.

All his life, Faraday kept notebooks in which he constantly recorded wild, poetic streams of thought and images that passed through his mind. He described whatever natural phenomena caught his eye, such as a rainbow held within a waterfall, but made no conscious connection between what he described and the complex scientific theories he evolved. His jottings were 'remarkably unsophisticated' according to Isaac Asimov. Faraday repeated himself and made no sense at all, with many incomprehensible scribbles. When scientists perused these notebooks, trying to understand the pattern behind his genius, they concluded that the very lack of organized thought showed that Faraday freely acknowledged what emerged into his mind. It was this very freedom that made him a visionary scientist in the truest sense of the word.

Basing his early experiments on an article in an encyclopedia, Faraday had taught himself the rudiments of electrochemistry. He was eventually apprenticed to the renowned chemist Sir Humphrey Davy, and moved into scientific research. At the time, scientists envisaged electricity as a fluid material that flowed through wires. Faraday envisioned it as a vibration or force transmitted through the conductor. Underpinning all his work was his notion of the unity of the forces of nature. He realized that space was not, as was thought, empty but was actually the medium through which magnetism and force passed. He pictured this as elastic bands spanning space. When the complicated mathematics needed to explain his concept were worked out by James Clerk Maxwell, Faraday wrote to him, begging him to 'put your hieroglyphs into the sort of common language that such as I could understand'. Nevertheless, it was Faraday's innovative thinking that led to modern electromagnetic field theory.

visualization

Visualization, a key tool of the intuitive mind, involves seeing
pictures as though projected on a screen, which may be inside your head
or a few feet in front of you.

Visualization is a form of visual thinking. In most people, these images go on all the time but are screened out. You can quickly learn to tune in. However, if you are not a visual person, and not everyone is, you can use your hands to help you in exercises. Formation of visual images can be helped, however, by looking up to your inner screen. This is located between and slightly above your eyebrows (the site of the metaphysical third eye). The act of raising your eyes triggers alpha waves and the visual part of the brain – which is useful whenever you are working with your intuition as it helps you to enter a relaxed state and to picture things. If you do this with your eyes closed, it enhances the images you want to access in guided visualization.

Connecting to the whole

Visualization and creative reverie are extremely effective ways to access your unconscious mind – a part of you that knows and which is connected into a greater whole. The unconscious mind is where enormous wisdom is stored and it contains knowledge that you have never actually learned.

RELATIVE VISUALIZATION

When Albert Einstein thought, he did so through imagery. Handicapped by a lack of language skills in his early years, he learned to access a stream of imagery instead. As he grew older, he let this image stream run freely while he observed its content. By imagining a train travelling at the speed of light, for example, and observing what he saw in his mind, he was able to formulate his complex theory of relativity – which arose out of his own intuitive powers rather than intellectual processes.

Music and the mind

Music helps images to form. Music that has been specially written for visualization or meditation is preferable as it will assist your brain to slip into the alpha and theta wave states that create the optimum conditions for visualization and intuition. Such music is often slow and soothing. However, it has been found that extremely complex music and progressive jazz can both stimulate images in the mind, but not necessarily intuition.

Music and relaxation

Music has a powerful effect on behaviour. Researchers at Ben-Gurion University in Israel have recently confirmed earlier findings by the RAC in England. They proved that drivers who listen to fast dance music or complex classical music, such as opera, while driving are twice as likely to have an accident. They have shown that music above 60 beats a minute, or with many notes and a crescendo–diminuendo – rising and falling – pattern, increases your heart rate and blood pressure – which is antagonistic to relaxation. On the other hand, music with less than 60 beats a minute actually lowers the heart rate and induces relaxation.

How to visualize

Struggling to visualize is counter-productive. The more you can relax and the more you can withdraw from the sensory input of the outside world, the more easily images will form. Choose a place that is free from distractions and is not too bright. Switch off your phone because there is nothing so irritating as an image beginning to focus and the ringing of the phone shattering it. If you find that there is a repetitive noise in the outer world, incorporate this into your

visualization, telling yourself that each time you hear it, you will relax more and more deeply.

When you begin visualization, try not to get too hung up on the details. Colours and directions are easily transposed because you are using a part of your brain that is not concerned with such details. Do not assume that you have got something wrong because the instructions say something else. It is your intuition that you are accessing, not mine. If you get a picture that is different to what an exercise says, work with that. It is an excellent sign that your intuition is communicating with you!

EXERCISE
In your mind's eye

To prove to yourself that you can use your mind's eye for visualization, ask a friend to read this list to you, slowly at first and getting faster. Notice where your eyes move as you picture each item. Close your eyes and picture the following:

A bright red ball
A bright yellow square
An orange triangle
A table
A chair
A table and chairs

Your childhood home
Your first school
Your desk
Your teacher
Your child
Your partner
Your mother
Your great-great grandmother
Your great-great grandchild
Your most unfavourite place
The surface of Mars
The centre of the earth

Very few people find this exercise impossible. A little challenging in parts perhaps, but the imagination fills in the blanks. In visualization, active imagination acts as a vehicle for intuition. Notice, too, whether your other senses come into play. Do you smell your unfavourite place – does your nose wrinkle with distaste, for instance?

EXERCISE
Your favourite place

Having proved to yourself that you can picture things, close your eyes and try the following exercise:

- Close your eyes and breathe gently. Slowly bring your attention into yourself and allow the outside world to fade away. If you hear noises, let them fade away. If you have thoughts, let them pass on by. Let your mind be quiet and calm.
- Now take yourself to your favourite place. Picture it, see the colours. Feel yourself there, notice its textures, smell the smell of the place, hear its sounds. Feel the temperature, the air on your skin, the ground beneath your feet. Enjoy this space. Rest and relax here, allow it to revitalize you. Let it bring you to a point of inner stillness.
- When you are ready to leave, open your eyes. The place to which you go will be the starting point for some of the guided journeys you will take as you work your way through this book.

Confirming visualization

Visualization does not depend on seeing images clearly. Many people say they cannot visualize and yet they react strongly, especially on a physical level, to visualization exercises. Brain scans show that people who are visualizing have exactly the same brain activity as they would if they were actually hearing or seeing something. When they try to imagine a picture, the visual cortex lights up. When they imagine a sound, the auditory cortex becomes active.

If you want to check whether you are visualizing or not, try the following exercise. If possible, have someone else read it to you while you sit with closed eyes. But if not, actively read the exercise, involving your feelings, making the movements, and really trying to picture it. If you get a reaction in your body, you are visualizing!

EXERCISE
Eating an apple

Sit comfortably. Now imagine that you are holding a ripe, green, juicy apple in your left hand. Feel its weight, its coolness and smooth roundness. In your right hand, you hold a knife. With this knife, peel the top of the apple. Then cut yourself a slice. You will feel the juice oozing out and smell the aroma of freshly peeled apple. Lift it up to your mouth. As you take a bite, you realize that it is a cooking apple, and is very sour and sharp.

You may well have found that you had a physical reaction and your mouth puckered from the sour taste as you read that exercise. If it did, you are visualizing even if you did not actually picture the apple. With more practice, images will form.

Aids to visualization

Crystals are extremely useful for inducing visualization. If you place a prehnite, azurite with malachite, or golden labradorite crystal on your third eye, visualization is sharper.

Many people say they cannot visualize and yet they react strongly, especially on a physical level.

creating a safe space

The purple pyramid meditation is a powerful tool that can be used to protect yourself or a room or a building during metaphysical work and when performing the intuitive exercises in this book.

The purple pyramid visualization has been in use at the very least since Ancient Egyptian times. It therefore has enormous power and is very effective. You can visualize a purple pyramid around your home and leave it in place permanently. It can also be used whenever you feel the need of protection – some people add wheels to their pyramid to make a mobile shelter that accompanies them wherever they go.

If you have difficulty visualizing, use your hands to mark out the space and place an amethyst pyramid in it, or make a paper pyramid and paint it purple. Kinaesthetic people find movement effective and should walk the sides of the pyramid on the floor and use their arms to go to the apex.

Picture an amethyst light coming in from the apex and shining all around the pyramid.

EXERCISE
The purple pyramid

- Sit comfortably, breathing gently. Close your eyes and look up to the space above and between your eyebrows.
- Imagine that you are sitting in the middle of a purple pyramid. It is made of amethyst crystal. Trace the outline of the pyramid with your mind or your hands, and see it in your mind's eye. Fill in the sides with purple light. The pyramid should have a floor under your feet and four sides that meet above your head.
- When the pyramid is strong, let it expand to encompass the room in which you are sitting, or the whole building.
- Take your attention up to the apex.
- Picture an amethyst light coming in from the apex and shining all around the pyramid. Let this light sweep out the pyramid, transmuting any negative energies into positive ones. Allow the light to revitalize the space within the pyramid. Amethyst is both protective and uplifting. Sitting in this pyramid will take you to the highest vibration possible while keeping you safe.
- Slowly bring your attention back into your body and be aware that you and the room – or house – are now protected by the purple pyramid. Take your attention down to your feet and re-earth yourself by picturing a cord going from the centre of each foot deep down into the earth, joining and passing through the base of the pyramid. Close the shields over your third eye.
- When you are sure you are fully grounded and back in your body, open your eyes and move around.

the grounding cord

*Having established your protection, the next step is to strengthen
the grounding cord that holds you in incarnation and keeps you in touch
with your body and the earth plane.*

Just as there is a physical umbilical cord to the mother, so there is a metaphysical umbilical cord to the spiritual mother, the earth. A cord goes from the soles of each foot and the two cords join together at the earth chakra, from where it passes deep into the earth, to keep the body in incarnation. This cord is flexible and does not hamper your movement, but it does help you to settle your consciousness back into your body when meditation or intuition exercises are complete. It can also help to 'reel you back' during an out-of-body experience or if you feel at all floaty at any time.

EXERCISE
Growing your grounding cord
• Stand or sit with your feet firmly on the floor and take your attention down to your feet. Close your eyes.
• Picture a cord growing from the centre of each sole of your feet, like a root. They pass into the centre of a flower (the earth chakra) and the two strands unite. The cord goes deep into the earth. It is flexible and allows you to move, but it holds you in incarnation.
• When you feel grounded in your physical body, close your third eye shields and open your eyes.

relaxation

Relaxation greatly aids both meditation and guided visualization,
and it has been proved to facilitate the development of intuitive powers.
It has great benefits for our health, too.

Practise the following relaxation exercise until you can completely relax quickly and easily whenever you undertake the intuitive practices in this book.

EXERCISE
Relaxation

• Settle yourself down in a comfortable place where you will not be disturbed. Breathe gently and easily. Raise and lower your eyelids ten times, then allow your eyes to remain closed. Your eyelids will feel relaxed and pleasantly heavy.

• Raise your eyebrows high and stretch your whole face. Relax and let go. Let the relaxed feeling from your eyelids travel slowly up your forehead and across your scalp, and through all your facial muscles. Smile as widely as you can, move your jaw from side to side, and allow your face to relax.

• Now lift your shoulders up to your ears and let go. Allow the relaxed feeling to flow on down through your body. Take a big breath and sigh out any tension you may be feeling. Let your chest and back relax and soften.

- Clench your fists and let them relax on your thighs. Allow the sense of relaxation that is passing through your body to go down your arms. Any tension that is left will drip out of your fingertips and trickle down to the earth.

- Pull your belly in, breathing deeply. Let all your breath out and count to ten. Allow your lower back and abdomen to feel warm and relaxed.

- Let the feeling of relaxation go on down through your thighs and knees, flowing down your legs to your feet. Raise and lower your feet and let your calf muscles be soft and loose. Scrunch your toes up and let them relax. Allow any tension left in your body, this to drain out of your feet.

- You will now be feeling comfortably warm and peaceful. Spend a few

moments enjoying this feeling of total relaxation. You will remain mentally alert but physically relaxed.

- When you have finished your relaxation, bring your attention back into your surroundings. Place your feet firmly on the floor and sit up straight. Be aware of your connection with the earth. Get up and move around.

'Upon his heart fell one drop of Brahmic bliss, leaving henceforth and always an aftertaste of heaven.'

Charles Tart, paraphrasing Richard Buckle

meditation

Regular meditation is an excellent way to expand intuition.
The type of meditation that does this is not one that concentrates on
a mantra or purely on the breath to empty the mind.

The form of meditation that is needed for intuition is not an 'empty mind' – that takes you beyond the place where images form and intuition expands. Intuitive meditation uses imagery but if you don't see pictures, let yourself feel things instead. What you are seeking is a quiet mind, an inner point of stillness, and a blank screen on which your intuition can write, rather than an empty mind.

Appropriate music can be extremely useful in helping you to relax and put aside thoughts of the day as it puts your mind into the right space. It is traditional to sit with a straight back for meditation, with your feet on the floor and your hands resting lightly on your thighs. Having your feet on the floor helps you when you want to end the meditation. However, if you find another position more comfortable, then adopt that pose. It is more important to be fully relaxed and free from distractions than to sit in the 'right' position.

The time to meditate

It is also traditional to meditate at the same time every day, but again it is more important actually to do the meditation each day rather than stick rigidly to a particular time. You may well find that you can quieten your mind more easily in the morning than the evening, or the other way round, in which case time your meditation accordingly.

Always choose a time to meditate when you will not be disturbed – take the phone off the hook or switch on the ansaphone and switch off your mobile. Allow yourself five or ten minutes every day when you begin, and gradually lengthen it to 15 or 20 minutes.

Passing thoughts

Initially you will probably find that many trivial thoughts pass through your mind. If this is the case, don't try to stop them, simply let them pass on through. In time the 'thoughts' that you have will be your intuition communicating with you. You may 'see' them as pictures in your mind's

eye, 'hear' them as an inner or outer voice speaking to you, or 'feel' them without knowing quite how it happened. All of these are equally valid ways, nothing is right or wrong. You have to find the way that is best for you.

calming the mind

Research has shown that the intuition functions best when outside stimulus is reduced to a minimum but the mind remains attentive and aware.

A still mind has always been the goal of Eastern meditation. As Krishnamurti explained: 'Clarity, insight or understanding are only possible when thought is in abeyance, when the mind is still. Then only can you see very clearly, then you can say you have understood, then you have direct perception.'

To achieve this absence of thought, concentration on the breath is often used. You sit and observe the gentle sensation of the breath entering your nostrils, passing down into your lungs and moving out again. This can be a useful way of moving out of everyday awareness into stillness.

With practice, it only takes a few moments to calm the mind and it is an exercise that can be performed anywhere. If you let your eyes go softly out of focus at the same time, sensory input is considerably reduced and you enter a state of attentive expectation. If you find that 'mind chatter' is a problem, try placing a blue selenite or rhomboid calcite crystal on your third eye or use the Bach flower essence White Chestnut.

Another way of calming the mind is to contemplate an image. Mandalas have been used for this purpose for thousands of years. They bring you to the point of stillness, the space in which you hear your inner voice.

intuitive meditation

*A guided journey makes an excellent starting point for intuitive meditation
as it leads you into a deeply relaxed yet attentive space that is conducive to
communication while keeping your mind occupied.*

EXERCISE
A guided journey

- Sit comfortably and close your eyes. Raise and lower your shoulders; as they drop, allow any tension to fall away. (If you need deeper relaxation see page 134.)
- Take your attention to the base of your spine. You have an energy point here which, when open, will stop you drifting away. You may feel it rotating like a wheel or sense energy pulsing there. If you feel yourself 'floating' or drifting too far away from contact with your body, take your attention to this point and it will bring you back.

- Begin by asking that your energies will be raised to the highest possible level and that any guidance you receive will come from the highest source.
- Establish a gentle rhythm of breathing, with the out breath slightly longer than the in breath. Pause between each in and out breath.
- Slowly bring your attention into yourself and allow the outside world to fade away. If you do hear noises, do not be disturbed by them. If you have thoughts, let them pass on by. Let your mind be quiet and calm.
- Now take yourself to your favourite

place. Picture it, see the colours. Feel yourself there, notice its textures, smell the smell of the place, hear its sounds. Feel the temperature, the air on your skin, the ground beneath your feet. Enjoy this space. Rest and relax here, allow it to revitalize you. Let it bring you to a point of inner stillness.

• If anything else happens, note it but do not focus on it for too long. Allow your mind to remain quiet and peaceful. If you drift off into inappropriate thoughts, gently bring yourself back to your favourite place but be open to the possibility of your intuition communicating with you. When you are ready to return, become aware of your body sitting in the chair and of your feet on the floor. Picture a cord going from your feet down into the centre of the earth, gently and flexibly holding you in your chair.

entering meditation with ease

When you go into meditation, you enter an alpha brainwave state and then move into theta. Remaining attentive and retaining some beta brainwaves helps you to process and remember the information.

If you find it difficult to enter a meditative state, play music that has been specially written to enhance meditation. This appeals to the right hemisphere of your brain, the intuitive and meditation-orientated side. The following exercises help you to slip into a meditative state quickly. See which one is the most effective for you and introduce it at the start of the exercises.

EXERCISE
The ball of light
Close your eyes and look up to the point above and between your eyebrows. Now take your awareness out a few feet in front of you. There is a ball of light here, like those in night-clubs. As it turns it flashes coloured lights out from the many facets on its shiny surface. Watch it turn, spinning faster and faster with the light flashing and sparkling, more and more light spinning off it, until it suddenly stops and leaves you in a peaceful space.

EXERCISE
The golden circle
Close your eyes and look up to the point above and between your eyebrows, focusing on your third eye. You will find

a small golden ball here. It is turning slowly. As you watch, it spins faster and faster, moving into your skull. It moves in a great flat circle all around the inside of your skull, level with your third eye. It is moving so fast that all you can see is a golden circle of light spinning inside your head, like a halo that has dropped down around your brain. When it slows down, it settles at a point exactly in the centre of the circle. This is your point of stillness. If you lose that point of stillness, go back to the spinning golden ball and let it settle in the middle again.

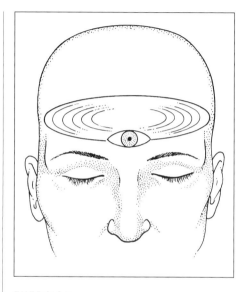

EXERCISE
Pointillion

Close your eyes and look up to the inner screen above and between your eyebrows. Using large black dots, write your full name on the screen, followed by the word 'relax', also in dots. Rub it off. Repeat.

EXERCISE
Closing down

When you want to close down visualization, picture shields closing over your third eye, or cover the spot with your hand, to act as a signal that the visualization is ended.

face clearing

If you consciously take your vibrations up to their highest levels before you begin meditation, and keep the energy centre at the base of your spine open to help you stay grounded, you should experience little difficulty, but problems can arise.

It is quite common for colours, eyes or faces to zoom in rapidly when you start to meditate; some of these faces can be unpleasant. Initially, allow them to be there, don't focus too hard and try not to become frightened. As time goes on, these shadowy faces may well resolve themselves into guides, in which case you will be able to communicate effectively with them, but you can dissolve them.

Face sources

Faces can appear from four sources – your intuition, your unconscious mind and archetypal memories, thought forms created by other people, and the dimensions close to the earth on which 'lost' or malicious souls may become trapped. If you are unfortunate enough to attract the unwanted attention of the souls who hang around the earth, you can use the power of your mind to 'rub them out' using a light wand or a bucket of old-fashioned whitewash. (Also, make sure you wear a black tourmaline crystal for protection.) These techniques also work for thought forms or faces that arise out of your own mind. However, lack of fear is your best tool. Notwithstanding, such faces, and the animals or 'part faces' that may appear during meditation, may be gifts in disguise. If you can slow the faces down – they often move very quickly – and check them out, from within your safe space, you may find that they are not as frightening as they may appear. You may be able to communicate with them. Guides or other helpers such as power animals often present themselves in this way. While it can be disconcerting to see a disembodied eye, the whole face may gradually be discerned.

Dealing with the faces

Opening your physical eyes and putting your hand over your third eye, and closing the third eye, should stop faces intruding. If the faces continue to bother you, or seem to be asking you for something, it would be wise to find someone who is experienced in such matters to help you.

THE LIGHT WAND

Imagine that you are holding in your hand a long, slim wand of light. At the push of a button, the wand sends out a shaft of brilliant light that immediately and harmlessly dissolves all it comes into contact with.

gatekeepers and intuitive gateways

In the esoteric view, everyone has a gatekeeper, who may be male, female or of indeterminate gender. The gatekeeper can help you unlock the secrets of your unconscious.

Metaphysically speaking, your gatekeeper is someone with whom you have travelled through aeons of time and whom you can totally trust, part of your greater soul group. But if you don't believe that there is anything outside this present life, you can look on your gatekeeper as part of your psyche.

Your gatekeeper has control of the gateways to your intuitive mind. Located around your head, these intuitive gateways allow a flow of energy between the physical and subtle levels of being. They are what enable you to make journeys out of your body and to pick up intuitive communications. If your intuitive gateways open and close at your will, they can prevent anything untoward happening to you during meditation or altered states of consciousness. If a gateway is stuck open you could suffer from psychic invasion, attachment, and the like. (The Bush Flower Essences Fringed Violet and Flannel Flower dropped or sprayed onto your intuitive gateways will help to bring them back under control.)

If you have used recreational or prescribed psychotropic drugs and have experienced 'flashbacks' or uncontrolled altered awareness, you may have blown your gateways and should not undertake the exercises in this book until they have been healed. Traditional Chinese acupuncture can help with this condition, as can the Aloha flower essence Painini-Awa'Awa rubbed on your head or dispersed through your biomagnetic field.

Trusting your gatekeeper

Getting to know your gatekeeper is one of the best ways to feel safe during any metaphysical work. When you trust your gatekeeper, you focus your intention on the work you are doing. Gatekeepers are often to be sensed standing behind you but they may make themselves known in other ways. You may experience a tingling on your scalp, a feeling of hands on your shoulders, sense a cloak or arms wrapped around you, or become aware of a particular perfume.

meeting your gatekeeper

*The following exercise will help you to get to know your gatekeeper
and to build up a bond of trust between you. Practise it regularly for a few
days until contact is automatic.*

EXERCISE
Bonding with your gatekeeper

- Settle yourself comfortably and quietly in a chair in a place where you will be undisturbed. Let your physical body relax and gently settle down. Breathe gently and bring your attention into yourself. If you have any thoughts that do not belong to this work, let them drift past. Do not focus on them.
- Take your attention to the top of your head and allow yourself to reach up mentally to the highest possible level. You may well feel that you are being

pulled up by a piece of string attached to the top of your head. If your head spins, take your attention down to the base of your spine and open the energy centre there. Then take your mind back up to the top of your head and around your shoulders.

- When you have reached up to the highest possible vibration, ask your gatekeeper to make him or herself known to you.
- Watch out for any unexplained feelings in or around your body – tingling, touch, movement of air, etc. You may receive a mind picture of your gatekeeper or have a sense of someone with you.
- Spend as long as you need getting comfortable with your gatekeeper. You may need to agree on a few ground rules for protecting your intuitive gateways. If so, negotiate these until

you are satisfied that your aims and those of your gatekeeper coincide.

- Ask your gatekeeper to show you where your intuitive gateways are. Check them out. Practise opening and closing them by visualizing them open and then closed.
- If you become aware that your intuitive gateways are stuck open, and anyone can access you or move in to influence you, ask your gatekeeper to help you bring these gateways back under your conscious control. To help this process, you can spray the Australian Bush Flower Essences Fringed Violet and Flannel Flower around your biomagnetic field. When you have completed the exercise, shut down your intuitive gateways. Then slowly bring your awareness back into your body and your attention back into the room.

the intuitive self

*Consciousness functions on many levels and there is far more
to a human being than first meets the eye. When you develop your intuition
you open up many layers of understanding.*

We are all reasonably familiar with the part of ourselves that is operating on the physical, emotional and mental levels. And most of us by now know that we have a subconscious mind which influences our behaviour without our knowing and which is home to fixed patterns and rigid expectations. Some of us understand the concept of the collective unconscious – the point where we all join at the level of the psyche, and which houses archetypes and myths. We may think we know ourselves as a spiritual being but what we often mean by that is someone who has religious or spiritual impulses or beliefs.

Few people are aware how much of them functions on a spiritual level. This is the 'intuitive self'. It is 'higher' because, like the subconscious mind, it functions on a

Few people are aware how much of them functions on a spiritual level.

different vibration to everyday awareness, although it pervades it. This vibration is finer, less dense, and therefore it extends beyond the purely physical. This is why your intuitive self can know so much more than your everyday self.

If you can raise your physical vibrations sufficiently to embody your intuitive self, to allow more of it down to manifest on the earth plane, you will automatically be more intuitive. The exercise on the next page should be taped, with appropriate pauses, or be read aloud by a friend, giving you plenty of time to carry out each instruction. Holding a selenite crystal in your hand will aid the process and you will have the crystal as a tangible reminder.

If you find raising your vibrations hard, imagine yourself getting into a lift, pressing the button marked 'top' and stepping out to be met by your intuitive self. Embody the intuitive self and return via the lift.

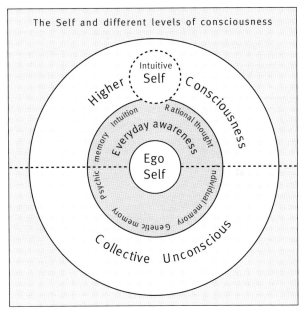

The Self and different levels of consciousness

Securing the intuitive self

Anchoring your intuitive self into the everyday physical realm makes accessing your intuition much easier. Practice this valuable exercise every day for at least a week, until you can do it instinctively.

EXERCISE

Embodying the intuitive self

- Make yourself comfortable and breathe gently and easily. Lift your shoulders up to your ears and let go. Take a big breath and sigh out any tension. Allow a sense of release to flow through your body.
- Take your awareness to your heart and the higher heart chakra located above it (you can touch them to focus your attention there). Allow them to unfold, opening like the petals of a flower. Then take your attention up to the crown chakra at the top of your head. Allow this chakra to open fully.

The chakras above your head will expand and you may feel a string pulling you up — allow yourself to go with this feeling. Consciously allow your vibrations to rise, to reach the highest possible level.

- Invite your intuitive self to move down through these chakras until it fills your crown chakra. From the crown chakra, feel your intuitive self enfold your whole body. Experience the love that your intuitive self has for you. Bask in its warmth, draw that love deep into your being.
- Spend time with your intuitive self,

welcoming it, learning to trust and feeling safe. (Take as long as you need at this point.)

• Then, when you are totally ready, bring your intuitive self into your heart chakras. Embody your intuitive self at the centre of your being. Enfold your intuitive self within your heart so that it is always accessible to you. Feel how different your body is when you embody your intuitive self – how protected you feel, how much more aware you are at an inner level as your vibrations are raised by the embodiment of your intuitive self.

• When you are ready to end the exercise, ask your intuitive self to remain with you, safely within your heart, and enfold your intuitive self within the heart chakras as you close them gently inward.

• Close the chakras above your head, letting them fold in on themselves like flowers closing for the night. Close the crown and third eye chakras and make sure that your earth chakra is holding you firmly in incarnation. Check that your grounding cord is in place. Slowly, bring your attention back to your physical body and the room around you and move around.

Spend time with your intuitive self, welcoming it, learning to trust and feeling safe.

meeting a mentor

Mentors come in many guises and can be inner or outer figures.
They may appear as people, animals, or otherworldly beings – and may
well change form. Their purpose is to assist you.

Mentors may be with you for a lifetime or during a specific task. If you have something you find difficult, you can request that a mentor be sent to assist. This can be useful if you have to find your way around a strange place or visit a country where you do not speak the language, for instance. But there are mentors that have advanced business acumen and others who offer innovative solutions or necessary skills.

Guidance and help

During one of my workshops, a woman 'saw' a Jesus-like figure as she waited for her mentor. 'Oh no,' she thought, 'I don't think I can be good enough to have you for a guide.' 'Is this better?' he asked, as he transformed his robe into a sweater and jeans. She found him much easier to relate to in his modern attire.

Unwanted aid

Sometimes people find that their mentor is someone they would rather not have assisting them. One woman, for instance, found that her mother-in-law arrived in her visualization. She had been a controlling figure when she was alive and the woman's heart sank at the thought of further control. So, she thanked her mother-in-law but tactfully explained that for the tasks over which she needed guidance someone with more specialized knowledge would be more appropriate, and added that she did not want to stand in the way of her mother-in-law's progression on the other side. Her mother-in-law was perfectly happy to leave the guiding to what she described as a 'higher being'. So bear in mind that you are in charge of this relationship.

MEETING A MENTOR

- Relax and take yourself into your favourite place. Ask that a mentor will come to you. Be expectant but not insistent. Have patience. Take time to walk around enjoying this beautiful space and the feeling of joyful anticipation this meeting invokes. As you walk around, you will become aware that someone is coming toward you. This is your mentor. Take all the time you need to get acquainted.
- When it is time to leave, thank your mentor for being there and arrange a call signal in case you need to get in touch. Your mentor will probably give you a recognition signal for future occasions. (If you are kinaesthetic or aural rather than visual, your mentor will make its presence known by touch, smell, words or an instinctive knowing.)

opening the inner senses

Opening the inner sense organs is the key to intuitive living.
It is not only during meditation that your intuition will speak to you;
it may help you at any time during your daily life.

A t every moment, it is necessary to be attuned to the whispered inner voice, the quiet feeling or the subtle clues glimpsed by the mind's eye. You need to develop the habit of paying instinctive attention to intuitive signals. Then bring them into focus and interpret them.

Introspective living

As Dr Paul Brunton explained: 'Such signs and tokens are shown us by the soul but they are often misunderstood or simply not noticed. They come quietly, as quietly as the sun steals into a darkened world, so quietly that [you are] likely to dismiss them as useless fantasies, meaningless thoughts or unimportant imaginings ….' The classic method of introspective enquiry which he and many occult schools taught is still effective today and only takes a minute or two of your time. At moments throughout the day, suddenly stop what you are doing, breathe gently and bring your attention quietly into yourself. Drop into the resulting silence a question, and wait with patient expectation for the answer to arise intuitively. The questions he suggests asking are: 'Who is doing this?', 'Who is feeling this emotion?', 'Who is thinking these thoughts?', 'Who is speaking these words?' This breaks up the illusion that the outer person is all that exists, and focuses you into your inner being. 'The practice of suddenly observing oneself, one's desires, moods and actions, is especially valuable because it tends to separate the thoughts and desires from the sense of selfhood that normally inheres in them, and thus tends to keep consciousness from being everlastingly drowned in the sea of five physical senses.'

The voice within

Practised regularly, this introspective enquiry moves you out of intellectual and emotional sensing, and into intuitive knowing. You no longer strive to achieve but rather seek to allow. The voice of the intuitive self will speak. You only have to listen for it.

TO OPEN THE INNER EYE AND EAR

During meditation it is common to see an eye opening or feel your ear pulsating – one ear, usually the left, rather than both. This can be deliberately extended to help your inner eye and ear open.

Picture an eye opening before you. Place this open eye on your third eye, and absorb it so that it passes through the skull and lodges behind your third eye.

Feel your ear pulsating with invisible sound. Move this pulsating ear back behind your physical ear.

practise to perfect

Practising intuition exercises as you go about your day-to-day business fills in those moments when you would otherwise be doing very little. Your intuition is like a muscle that responds well to exercise.

Left or right?

As you drive, try to anticipate whether the car ahead of you will turn left or right at a forthcoming junction.

Waiting for the mail

As you wait for your mail, close your eyes and try to anticipate who will be writing to you today and what they will say.

Answering the telephone

Before you pick up the phone, take a moment to tune into who will be on the other end and what they have to communicate to you.

Waiting for the train

If you travel to work by train, intuit exactly what time it will arrive each day.

Colours

Keep a pack of playing cards with you. Whenever you have a few moments, take them out, shuffle them face down. Before you turn each card up, foresee what colour it will be.

Anticipating traffic lights

As you watch traffic lights, try to anticipate the exact moment they will change colour.

Waiting for the elevator

As you wait for the elevator to arrive, intuit which floor numbers it will stop at on its way.

Watching the cursor

As you sit at your computer waiting for those boxes to pop up, position your cursor exactly where you expect it will need to be.

People watching

When in a restaurant or travelling on a train, pick a person and try to anticipate what their next move will be.

What comes next?

Tune into conversations going on around you. Try to anticipate what someone will say next. (Asking what comes next in any situation is a useful way to flex intuition.)

Who am I meeting?

If you have a friend to see or a business meeting, ask yourself exactly what they will be wearing today. Close your eyes and let a picture float into your third eye.

What comes next

Next time you have the radio on, try to forehear the next song to be played.

Tune into conversations going on around you. Try to anticipate what someone will say next.

the downside of intuition

*It would be irresponsible to pretend that intuition is purely sweetness and light.
Unfortunately, as everyone who is intuitive knows, the nastier side of life sometimes
makes itself known in advance and when it does, the effect can be unpleasant.*

The good news is that the more honed and skilful your intuition becomes, the less impact the nasty stuff has – and the more accurate and precise the information about such events becomes. You will no longer be prey to overwhelming premonitions of doom and gloom.

Whereas without trained intuition you may become disturbingly aware of an impending disaster, with it you will recognize what is about to happen and will know what can be done to meet it in the most constructive way possible. With foresight, it may be possible to circumvent the event altogether, but this is not always so. Sometimes we need the challenging events in our life to put us on another path. But, with foresight, you can face the challenge with an intuitive plan of action and on-going guidance and make the best of whatever situation comes your way.

Unwelcome news

As all professional psychics know, seeing death is one of the greatest dilemmas. It can be an extremely upsetting thing to hear, especially if it turns out not to be literally true. Death may signify an ending or a change. It does not necessarily mean a physical death. If it does, however, being prepared helps brings equanimity to the situation.

Training the intuition

Many people who foresee death feel guilty about it, as though they were somehow to blame for having caused it. Many years ago, before I had trained my intuition, I subconsciously tuned into the imminent death of a friend's father with whom he had had a major row. I urged Anthony to ring his father, who was travelling to another country, saying that it was important he phoned before his father left. Anthony insisted that he would ring the following month when he had the results of an important examination he was taking.

He rang me from an airport, saying that his father had had a stroke as he stepped off the plane and was now in hospital. Anthony was on standby. 'Don't worry,' I said, 'You will get there in time. It will be all right.' I could not have stopped those words from coming out of my mouth, and I had no knowledge of what I would say. When Anthony arrived at the hospital his father briefly regained consciousness and they were able to resolve their differences

There are times when you can do nothing except register and record what you see and let it go.

before he died. When Anthony phoned to tell me the news, he said: 'You knew, didn't you. You must have known because you kept telling me to phone.' It was useless trying to explain that while I had known he needed to phone, I had no idea of why, and it took some time to get over the feeling of guilt that arose.

Handling unwanted precognition

Nowadays I would still urge someone to phone in similar circumstances but I would have a much clearer knowing of why I felt it was so important. I would explain that, while I felt an ending was coming, it need not necessarily be a death. But, because of all that I have learned about the process of death, I would also offer, if the person was receptive, some guidance about the best way to help someone make the transition and how to keep intuitive contact with them as they passed into another dimension. And I would certainly not feel guilty. Fore-knowledge can be a wonderful thing as it can turn the most negative event into a positive happening.

Nevertheless, there are times when the events that premonitions foretell cannot be turned around and there will be times when the predicted events, personal or public, do not materialize. (Many more predictions turn out to be untrue than true, it is not an exact science even for the most skilful psychic and there are alternative realities.) Even when the details are clear, the timing or precise location may be difficult to ascertain. There are times when you can do nothing except register and record what you see and let it go. As your intuition offers more information, it is important to learn how to handle the capricious wildness of uninvited precognition.

DEALING WITH PREMONITIONS OF DOOM

- Stop, sit down, and let your eyes go out of focus. Slow your breathing down and relax. If you have just awakened from a dream, sit up.
- Take your attention into your solar plexus. Clarify what you are sensing or have dreamt, finger dowsing if needed.
- Ask: 'Is this premonition valid and real?'
- If the answer is no, picture white light surrounding your biomagnetic field, dissolving the experience. Open your eyes and proceed no further.
- If the answer is yes, ask for precise details. Who is involved? What will happen? Why is this occurring? When?
- Ask if there is anything you can do. Do you need to say anything to anyone? Is it preventable?
- If the answer is no, write up the premonition in your Intuition Journal. Ask that universal light and love will be sent to the situation. Get up and walk away from it. Your intuition has told you there is nothing more you can do. Remind yourself that you are not responsible for what you see – you are, however, responsible for how you deal with it.
- If the answer is yes, ask for precise guidance. What do you need to do? Who do you talk to? What do you say? When do you need to say or do it?
- Be sure to take any action necessary, or pass on exactly what you are told. Do not inflate it or agonize about it. Put it aside, let it go.

Projection and wishful thinking

Projection occurs when your own fears and expectations subtly influence what you intuitively see or sense. It also occurs when what you refuse to face in yourself is 'seen' in the people around you. So, for instance, everyone has an inner terrorist who could wreak terrible destruction. This can contaminate what you sense in the world around you, so that many of the doom-laden scenarios that an untrained intuitive apparently perceives are actually coming out of their own subconscious mind. Projection affects trained psychics too.

Wishful thinking can likewise colour perception. If you intensely wish for something to happen, you may believe that your intuition is telling you it will occur when it is actually your own overpowering desire or your ego at work. Facing up to your fears, accepting and integrating the qualities of your shadow self, and learning to recognize and control intense desires will help you to 'clean up' and refine your intuition.

Precognition and disaster

As might be surmised, there were many psychics who claimed to have foreseen the events of September 11. A British man, Chris Robinson, dreamed the event intensely on several occasions in August 2001 while being tested by Professor Gary E. Schwartz of the University of Arizona. On September 9, two days before the attack occurred, Robinson wrote to the US Embassy in London to warn them an aircraft was to be used by terrorists as a weapon of destruction against a tall building in New York.

Another Briton, Dave Mandell, drew a graphic representation of the destruction of the twin towers by an aircraft – which he dreamed five years to the day before it occurred. Mandell took his drawing to the local bank and was photographed in front of a calendar and witnesses. Six months later he had to repeat the process when he again dreamed of the twin towers splitting apart, with great chunks falling off them before one of the towers started to topple. This was not the first precognitive dream Mandell had received – he also predicted events such as Concorde crashing, a boat sinking and numerous earthquakes, floods and assassinations.

An English psychic, Valerie Clark, appeared on BBC TV's 'Kilroy' programme three months before September 11. She described a disturbing vision she had had several years previously in which she was wandering around during bombing of the World Trade Centre and saw a plane going past. She was, however, unclear whether it went into the building or not. After the September 11 disaster she was convinced that this was what her dream had foretold. Hindsight is, of course, infallible.

Real life often emulates fiction. Stephen King, writing as Richard Bachman, ended his story *The Running Man* by the hero crashing an empty plane into the plate-glass window of a tall tower out of which a media boss, who had double-crossed him, was staring. The media man's last sight was the hero giving him the finger. It could be deemed to be prophetic, although the details are far from exact, but it could also be the writer reaching into the zeitgeist to pluck out a suitable revenge. Then again, it could be skilful use of a vivid imagination.

Levels of consciousness

When you open your intuition, especially when you begin to meditate, you often find that you go into 'peak experiences', what the Buddhists call bliss or enlightenment and other disciplines call cosmic consciousness or wholeness. Such

THE WHITE LINER

In 1898 Morgan Robertson, an American science-fiction writer, described the wreck of a gigantic white ship, the Titan. Measuring 800 feet long and displacing 70,000 tons, it carried 3,000 passengers. Its engine had three propellers. On its maiden voyage one night in April, it hit an iceberg in fog and sank.

The liner Titanic was 828 feet long, displaced 66,000 tons, had space for 3,000 persons and was fitted with three propellers. It too hit an iceberg.

When you open your intuition, especially when you begin to meditate, you often find that you go into 'peak experiences', what the Buddhists call bliss or enlightenment and other disciplines call cosmic consciousness or wholeness.

experiences are expansive — light floods in, the inner world becomes the outer world, the outer world the inner. When the painter Vincent Van Gogh had such a vision, the starry night he was observing metamorphosed. The stars turned into enormous whirlpools of light and energy and the trees flamed toward the heavens.

But, as so often happens, Van Gogh crashed into the deepest despair. He was experiencing two opposite polarities, bliss and despair, bouncing between the extremes of higher and lower consciousness. The peak and the despair are experiences, but many people confuse them with emotions. Physiologically, endorphins are characteristic of bliss states, adrenalin of the pits. If too much adrenalin is produced over a long period of time, it has a detrimental effect on physiological and psychological health, so you need to learn how to control your fear response.

Controlling fear

In the 'pit' state of lower consciousness fear rushes in. The lower levels of consciousness tend to take over at night. You wake up, heart pounding. You find yourself hot, dizzy, unable to breathe.

Adrenalin is pumping round your system. This is when you have intimations of doom. You will doubtless hope when you go to bed that it won't happen again, but of course it does because you have given it attention and the brain does not understand 'not'. When you learn to switch this response off, life stabilizes. You still experience the moments of bliss, but the fear recedes.

Positive thinking

To control fear fully, you also need to be aware of your negative thoughts. Everyone has about 55,000 thoughts a day (that's about as many as there are words in this book). Many of them are negative and you need to switch them to positive. The technique for stopping negative thoughts dead in their tracks is the same as for switching off adrenalin. Negative thoughts create what you most fear because you come to expect it. And, as the brain does not understand the word 'no', telling yourself it will not happen is counter-productive. What you have to do is learn to catch the thought before it happens or the adrenalin reaction before it is switched on.

The thought police

As soon as you become aware that you are having a negative thought, stop. Mentally take a step back, erasing the thought as you do so. Have a positive thought and move forward with it.

To help you catch those unwise thoughts, you can create a thought policeman or woman who will tap you on the shoulder and say 'stop' a moment before the thought comes into your mind. Picture it happening two or three times, and then leave your subconscious mind to carry on.

EXERCISE
The adrenalin controller

In your brain there is a switch marked 'Adrenalin On/Adrenalin Off'. In charge of this switch is a controller. The controller switches the adrenalin on whenever you get worked up, stressed or fearful, whether or not the situation warrants it.

In your mind, picture this switch. Set it to 'Off' and tape it into position. Inform the controller that it is now in charge of making sure no one interferes with the switch. It is the controller's job to keep it in the 'Off' position and to shout 'Stop' before you go into fear mode. The controller is responsible for keeping you happy and healthy.

Changing perspective

Fearfulness and lower states of consciousness can be likened to a worm who has popped his head above the earth. He cannot see very much – just a few blades of grass, a worm cast or two he left behind last time he was here. He has no idea of the bigger picture and he cannot see what is coming or what might happen. At any moment a blackbird might pull him from the ground.

Higher consciousness and intuitive states are like a bird's-eye view. The overview is there, the bigger picture, and yet the eye can focus in on the smallest detail. If you get into the habit of seeing the world from the bird's-eye view rather than the worm's eye view, life takes on a very different look.

EXERCISE
View of the eagle

This simple exercise helps you to shift perspective. Practise the exercise regularly until it becomes instinctive.

In your mind's eye become a worm. Feel yourself wriggling your head out above the grass, smell the moist, earthy smell, see the grass in front of you, and try to see beyond it. Now become an eagle soaring high overhead. Feel the air slide past your wings. Let your eyes see the bigger picture. Then focus on the worm. Now pull back and see the bigger picture. Promise yourself that you will see life with an eagle's eye from now on.

Higher consciousness and intuitive states are like a bird's-eye view.

Chapter six

In two minds

'... ideas about the nature of consciousness and the relationship between consciousness and matter (particularly the brain) have to be radically revised. It is my firm belief that we are rapidly

approaching a point
when transpersonal psychology
and the work with non-ordinary
states of consciousness
will become integral parts of
a new scientific paradigm
of the future.

Professor Stanislav Grof, *Thinking Beyond the Brain* (2001)

mind, brainwaves, consciousness

While it is clear that intuition is a function of the mind,
it is far from clear whether, as many scientists would like to believe,
it is actually generated by the brain.

Metaphysicians would agree with Willis W. Harman, Professor of Engineering-Economic Systems, Stanford University when he says: 'Mind is not brain.'

However, it is apparent that the brain mediates what happens to intuition as all communication goes through the brain to be turned into speech, sight, body awareness and feelings.

Imaging the brain

With the sophisticated imaging equipment now available, neuroscientists are able to pinpoint the parts of the brain involved in intuitive activities. But that does not mean they are able to explain them fully. For instance, when research was carried out into brainwave activity during past-life regression, it was found that not only did the regression therapist's brain synchronize with the patients, but also that simultaneous beta and delta waves were present – a situation that, according to orthodox science, does not occur, and yet researchers have monitored other combined states during meditation and dreams.

Four types of brainwave frequencies have, so far, been identified – beta, alpha,

theta and delta. Beta is present in the waking state during everyday awareness and when processing information. It is also present, in combination with other brainwaves, during lucid dreaming and precognition.

Universal awareness

Alpha occurs during meditation and altered states of awareness such as dreams and imaging. Theta also occurs during deep meditation. Delta is produced in dormant states. It is a form of universal awareness and taps into what Rupert Sheldrake has called 'the morphogenic field' and mystics 'the universal mind'. It is not present during 'ordinary' dreams but is present in extrasensory experiences such as precognition and out-of-body states and seems to act as a bridge to higher knowledge. If you are purely in theta mode, however, you will not remember anything about your experiences when you return to everyday awareness.

It is clear from biofeedback techniques that it is possible to train the brain to maintain or attain certain brainwave combinations, and this would be a fruitful area for research and development of intuition. When leading-edge imaging equipment is applied to the brain during psi-states and so-called paranormal activities, it may well be that it will locate the exact sites in the brain where

Alpha occurs during meditation and altered states of awareness such as dreams.

precognition and the like are processed. It is likely that, like a muscle, this site is present in everyone but, as with someone who exercises a muscle daily, it will be more strongly developed and visible in intuitives. Researchers are already aware that people who use their memory a great deal have a much more extensive 'memory' area in the brain – to the extent that adjacent sites are often taken over.

Brain patterns in psychic dreams

When psychic dreamer Chris Robinson was tested by Professor Gary E. Schwartz of the University of Tuscson, Arizona, he spent ten nights wired up in a sleep laboratory to test his brainwave patterns. During his precognitive dreams, his patterns were different to anyone else who had been tested there. Robinson had the kind of paroxysms or discharges that

MIND LINK

Research has shown that when minds are in rapport, they do not have to be in the vicinity to synchronize. A person was isolated in a remote location and wired up to an EEG machine to measure brainwave patterns. The research partner was subjected to intermittent strobe lighting and a careful note of time kept. The person at the remote location showed brainwave changes that accorded exactly with those strobe lights. Despite the fact that there were no visual or auditory clues when the strobe light was flashing, the brain waves were synchronized.

would normally be seen in epilepsy. The anomaly is being closely monitored but may well point the way forward for researchers to understand exactly what does go on in the brain during precognition.

The right and left brains

While all metaphysicians would assert that consciousness is not confined to the brain, one part of the brain is in fact orientated toward intuition. The human brain has four parts to it – the left and right hemispheres and the front and rear brains. The rear brain is the oldest, holding both personal and collective memories, and is concerned with autonomous bodily functions such as breathing.

The left and right hemispheres are concerned with different ways of thinking and perceiving the world. The left brain thinks in straight lines, the right in starbursts. One side of the brain, the right, is imaginative, intuitive and, like a muscle, can be strengthened with use, which is what this book is all about.

Left- or right-brained

How you communicate is closely related to which hemisphere of your brain is the

The left and right hemispheres are concerned with different ways of thinking and perceiving the world.

more active. Left-brained people are precise and organized, whereas right-brained people tend to be more visual and creative. The hands often do the talking when words fail the right-brained person, and they frequently confuse left and right. The left hemisphere is logical and rational. Where the right brain will make a huge intuitive leap and rarely knows how it got its result, the left brain reasons things through a step at a time. The left side of the brain dislikes complexity and ambiguity, the right side thrives on it.

If you are left-handed, you are far more likely to use your right brain (the right hemisphere controls the left side of the body), and this in turn may affect your career. Many musicians, artists and actors are right-brain dominant and 40 per cent of architects are left-handed. This is not surprising as it is the right brain that handles geometry and spatial awareness.

LEFT BRAIN	RIGHT BRAIN
Logical	Illogical
Linear	Random
Sequential	Simultaneous
Rational	Creative
Analytic	Synthetic
Verbal	Non-verbal
Time-orientated	No time concept
Relies on sensory input	Does not need sensory input
Mathematical/digital	Spatial

Relates to

Linguistics	Music and the arts
Intellectual processes	Feelings and emotion
Syntactical language	Imagery
Categories	Integral wholes
Boundaries	Unity

left- or right-brain dominance

Assessing which side of your brain is most active, whether you are 'left-brained' or 'right-brained', helps you to compensate for any imbalance and to activate your intuition.

Most people use one side of their brain rather more than the other, although some people have balanced hemispheres. If you use your right brain, you will be artistic, perceptive and feeling-orientated. Visualization will be easy. You will resonate to metaphors and myths, which gives you a head start when it comes to communicating with your intuition.

To assess which brain hemisphere you use, stop reading now and tick the appropriate boxes on the opposite page. If you tick mostly boxes on the left-hand columns, you are left-hemisphere orientated and may need to develop your intuitive side more by painting your feelings, writing stories and other right-brain activities. If you tick more boxes on the right-hand columns, you are right

If you use your right brain, you will be artistic, perceptive and feeling-orientated.

hemisphere orientated. You may well be intuitive already, but find it hard to function in the practical world. Making lists is an excellent way to bring more balance into your brain.

Equal numbers of boxes indicate that your hemispheres are balanced. This means that you can easily access your intuition and put it to work in a practical way. (In some people, particularly those who are left-handed, the hemispheres may be reversed – the brain is wired up differently. A following exercise will reveal whether this is true for you.)

ARE YOU LEFT- OR RIGHT-BRAINED?
Tick the boxes that best describe your thinking processes:

Left	Right	Left	Right
Linear ❑	❑ Holistic	Time-orientated ❑	❑ Outside time
Word-orientated ❑	❑ Visual, non-verbal	Sequential ❑	❑ Boundless
Logical ❑	❑ Non-rational	Abstract ❑	❑ Spatially perceptive
Analytical ❑	❑ Looking for synthesis	Categorical ❑	❑ Insightful
Pedantic ❑	❑ Open-minded	Theoretical ❑	❑ Experiential
Intellectual ❑	❑ Imaginative	Goal-oriented ❑	❑ Process-oriented
Practical ❑	❑ Idealistic	'Masucline' ❑	❑ 'Feminine'
Symbolic ❑	❑ Metaphoric	List-oriented ❑	❑ Confuse left and right
Judgemental ❑	❑ Feeling-orientated	Hands stay still ❑	❑ Hands do the talking

understanding brain function

These simple exercises will reveal whether your left or right hemisphere is dominant, or whether you are equally balanced. It is useful to have a friend read the donkey exercise to you, or tape it yourself with pauses.

Exercise
Touring the brain

Close your eyes and relax. Take your attention into your brain. Move around it, left to right. Does your brain feel bigger or more active on one side than the other? Is one side lighter than the other, or emptier? Does energy radiate from one side only? Are both sides of your brain equal?

Make a mental shopping list of the things you need to buy next time you are at the store. Notice which side of your brain is active. Now think of a point which is moving inward, tracing a spiral pattern. Visualize it in your mind's eye. The point moves from just inside your skull to deep within your brain. Which side of your brain feels active?

During these exercises, one side of your brain may well feel more active than the other. If the left side is dominant, you will have found it much easier to write the mental shopping list than to trace the spiral – unless your hemispheres are crossed (in this case, the right-hand side will have felt more active). If the right side is stronger, you will have struggled to write the list and, most probably, promptly forgotten most of it.

EXERCISE

Where's the donkey?

Settle yourself comfortably. Close your eyes and look above and between your eyebrows. Onto your inner screen a picture of a field is being projected. It is a lush green field with plenty of grass and wild flowers. Across the centre of the field, from one side to the other, is a worn earth path. On this path walk a man and a donkey. Notice which side they enter from, and which way do they walk. Now bring your attention back into the room.

If the man and donkey entered from the right-hand side, you are left-hemisphere dominant. If they came from the left, you are right-hemisphere dominant. If they appeared in the middle, your hemispheres are trying to unite and are almost balanced. If you could see the field but not the donkey your hemispheres are equally balanced.

brain synthesis

Balancing the brain hemispheres is achieved by activities that stimulate the under-used side. If you are a dreamy right-brained person, make lists, do your accounts, read a map or write a business letter.

If you are a pragmatic left-brained person, you can deliberately choose a right-brained way of expressing yourself to stimulate this side of the brain. Listen to music, daydream, write an imaginative story, or draw with your eyes shut. Left-brained people tend to find it hard to express emotions. If you draw, using colours and patterns, you will be able to access your feelings more easily.

The Australian Bush Flower Essence Bush Fuchsia is excellent for integrating the hemispheres. You can also visualize your hemispheres into balance by practising the following exercise twice daily for a week.

EXERCISE
Balancing the hemispheres
Trace a line down the middle of your head, from your forehead to the back of your head and back again. The two hemispheres unite immediately below this line. Imagine a zigzag line of light moving from the front of your head to the back, stitching together the two halves of your brain and stimulating the neural pathways between the hemispheres. Picture the light flashing backward and forward across the pathways, uniting the different parts of your brain. Let the light continue until both sides feel balanced.

CHAPTER seven

Protection

'We are surrounded by a host of unseen vibrations, a field of invisible energies, many of which can subtly affect our sense of well-being – and our ability to protect ourselves psychically.'

Judy Hall, *The Way of Psychic Protection*

protection

*Knowing how to protect yourself while working intuitively gives
you the confidence to work more openly and at deeper levels. It also helps
you to release unwanted vibes or feelings.*

A healthy biomagnetic field naturally acts as a protection during metaphysical work. The biomagnetic field is often known as the 'energy body' because of its vital and energetic appearance. Emotions and thoughts affect the colour of your biomagnetic field. A strong biomagnetic field is essential. If there are 'holes' or weak spots, energy can penetrate, or be drawn out from, your force-field (this can be healed, see page 83). In an emergency, you can gain instant protection by imagining that the outside edge of your biomagnetic field has crystallized – turned into a light-refracting crystal coating that neutralizes anything untoward. Your attitude will also affect how well protected you are.

• The first rule of protection when working with intuition is to banish fear. Metaphysics teaches that like attracts like and fear attracts undesirable entities and energies. If you have no fear, you will not need protection. If you have learnt to protect yourself, you have no need to fear. Working only at the highest possible vibration automatically protects you – as does practising with both discernment and discrimination.

- The second rule of psychic protection is to retain your common sense. So much that passes for 'intuitive guidance', 'channelling' and the like is at best rubbish and at worst misleading and sometimes downright dangerous. If your intuition or inner voice ever seems to be suggesting that you should harm yourself or others in any way whatsoever, it is safe to assume that this is not coming from a good space, nor is it for your highest good. We all have inner figures that sabotage us and there are beings on other planes of existence that, unfortunately, delight in misleading the gullible.

So, it is essential to know where your guidance is coming from, to ensure that you can close down at will, and to be able to filter out anything undesirable. Discernment, together with appropriate exercises and tools, makes protection an instinctive act. Working at the highest possible level in a safe and protected space (see page 130) ensures that you will receive only wise counsel.

metaphysical first aid

Use these quick fixes to resolve short-term problems or until you can put a permanent solution in place. They are all effective and easy to use and will help you deal with many difficult situations.

Picked up something nasty?

- Take a shower (visualize a shower of light if no water is available).
- Wear a piece of amber or black tourmaline.
- Wash your hands.
- Spray yourself with the flower remedy Crystal Clear.
- Comb your biomagnetic field with a selenite or quartz crystal.

Psychic vampirism

- Cross your ankles and place your arms over your solar plexus.
- Strengthen your biomagnetic field.
- Imagine cutting energy cords with a large pair of gold scissors.

To ward off psychic attack

- Get into your purple pyramid.
- Wear a black tourmaline.

Place a mental mirror between yourself and your attacker.

- In your imagination, electrify the edges of your biomagnetic shield.
- Place a mental mirror between yourself and your attacker.

Negative emotions/bad vibes

- Wrap yourself in mental light.
- Carry an apache tear in your pocket or wear one round your neck.
- Crystallize the edges of your biomagnetic field.
- Close and protect your chakras.
- Call on your guardian angel.

Unwanted channelling

- Close and protect your crown chakra.

Out of body

- Think yourself back or reel yourself in.
- Anchor your grounding cord deep in the earth.
- Move your physical body.

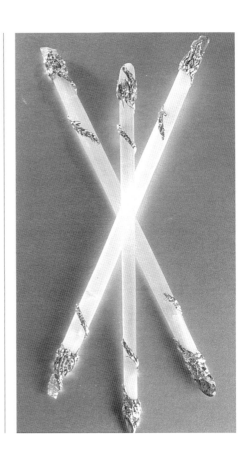

instant protection

*For instant protection, you can create a barrier of light around
you and a shield to neutralize negative energies. You also need a filter,
something that will screen out the rubbish.*

If you practise the following exercises until they are automatic, protection will be there when you need it.

EXERCISE
The psychic shield
Picture yourself entirely surrounded and enclosed by light (you may find it easiest to start with a light over your head and bring this down around your body, working toward your feet). Make sure that the light bubble goes under your feet and seals itself there. In one hand, visualize a silver shield that pulsates with light. Placing this shield between yourself and

anything doubtful or dangerous will neutralize the energy.

You can also 'crystallize' the outer edges of the bubble for additional protection. Visualize yourself standing inside a large, hollow crystal that is filled with light.

If you are kinaesthetic, use your hands to outline your biomagnetic field and feel it surrounded by light or use a candle flame or torch. Allow it to crystallize.

EXERCISE
The filter
Picture yourself entirely surrounded by a silver space suit. This space suit has a

communication panel on the front which
has been programmed to let only truth
communicate with you. If you press the
green button on the panel, you will be
able to hear – and see – what is being
communicated to you in truth. If you do
not hear or see anything, you will know
that what was being communicated to
you can be disregarded.

If you are kinaesthetic, touch your
hand to your chest, just below your
throat. As you touch this place, say out
loud 'I now touch the place of truth,
everything I hear or sense will be truth.

When you no longer need the filter,
take your space suit off and put it away
safely until you need it again. Remember
to close your third eye shield and to
check on your grounding cord and earth
chakra. If what you are hearing is negative
and damaging, press a red button to cut
off and erase the communication at once.

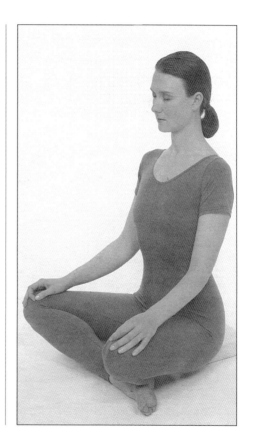

guardian angels

Guardian angels appear in literature that is at least five thousand years old.
Invoked for protection, an angel is a powerful guardian for the soul who is
journeying beyond the body and at all times when the intuitive faculties are open.

Guardian angels have traditionally been used down through the centuries for protection and guidance. Whether you regard them as external figures with an objective existence of their own, or as an embodiment of your own internal subjective reality, does not matter. They are valid and useful beings to bring into your life. Not all guardian angels, however, appear in traditional garb. You are just as likely to find that your guardian angel wears jeans and a sweatshirt as a robe and wings. You do not necessarily need to 'see' a guardian angel to know that one is there.

If you are primarily kinaesthetic, ask that you be given signals and feelings around your body.

Meeting a guardian angel

• Close your eyes. Spend a few moments relaxing, breathing gently and evenly, and letting any tension flow out of your body through your hands and feet.

• When you are ready, picture a shaft of light in front of you. This shaft of light reaches from the angelic realms straight down to earth. Ask that a guardian angel will travel this shaft of light to meet you.

• When your angel arrives, feel it move to stand behind you, wrapping you in protective wings or arms (not all angels have wings!). Spend as long as you like with your angel, building up trust and enjoying the sense of protection. Ask your angel to be with you whenever you feel you need protection. Silently affirm to yourself that this will be so.

• Ask your angel to show you a 'call sign', something you only need think about to have your angel present. Ask your angel to leave and then practise calling a few times so that you know that your angel will respond and come when you have need.

• Then thank your angel for being there. The shaft of light will recede back to the angelic realms.

• Before opening your eyes, take your attention down to your feet. Feel them firmly on the floor. Close your third-eye chakra shield. Then, when you are ready, bring your attention fully back into the room and open your eyes.

the inner saboteur

Saboteurs are inner figures who subtly obstruct your purpose or trip you up. They have been created at some time in your past, often during childhood, and have had a protective function.

Unfortunately, when you outgrew the need for that particular help, you did not necessarily outgrow the figure, who became lodged in your subconscious mind and still tries to 'keep you safe'.

If you find it difficult to develop your intuition, it could well be a saboteur that lies at the root of the problem. Children are extremely intuitive – until adults tell them it is all nonsense. They have to make the difficult decision between being intuitive or being rational. If your saboteur was formed during this process, it could well be 'keeping you safe' by blocking your intuition. Meeting this figure and explaining that you have matured and now have different needs will usually release the sabotage, and the figure may well be persuaded to take a more constructive part in your inner life from now on.

If you accept reincarnation and past lives, you may well find that the prohibition against being intuitive goes back to a time when you were persecuted for your gifts. Reminding yourself that you are now in a new incarnation and then communicating this information to the saboteur figure can release this prohibition and allow you to move on.

EXERCISE
Meeting the saboteur

- Sit quietly and let yourself relax. Take yourself to your favourite place. Spend a few moments enjoying being in this space. Walk around and enjoy its unique feel.
- When you are ready to seek the inner saboteur, look at what is beneath your feet in your favourite place. You will see that there is a trap door in front of you. Open this trap door and descend the ladder below – remember to take a light with you or look for a light switch as you go down the ladder.
- This is where your inner saboteur lives. This figure may be reluctant to come out into the light and may prefer to stay in a dark corner. If this is the case, try to reassure it and coax it into the light so that you can communicate more easily.

- Ask the figure what purpose it serves. (Wait quietly and patiently for the answer, do not push.)
- You will probably find that the figure once had a positive purpose but that this has changed over the years. If so, thank it for its care and concern and explain how things are different now.
- Ask the saboteur if it will help you by taking a more positive role in your inner life.
- If the answer is yes, discuss this and ask for a new name to go with its new role. If the answer is no, ask the saboteur if it is willing to leave you and take up residence somewhere where it will not frustrate your purpose. (You may need to do some negotiating here. Most saboteurs eventually agree to become more positive or to leave. If yours absolutely

refuses, it may need a different approach under the guidance of someone qualified in dispossession techniques.)

• When you have completed your discussions or negotiations, leave by the ladder and close the trap door. The figure may well come with you and can be encouraged to find an appropriate place to settle. (If the saboteur has been particularly obstreperous, sending it to outer space for the duration could be a solution.)

• When you are ready, open your eyes. Take your attention down to your feet and feel your feet on the earth.

• Be aware that your feet are connected to the earth, grounding you. Picture a shield closing over your third eye. With your eyes wide open, take a deep breath and stand up with your feet firmly on the earth. (If you are non-visual, take your mind around your body and allow yourself to feel intuitively where your inner saboteur lurks. Communicate through sensing, asking the same questions as above.)

• You can adapt the exercise to meet other inner figures, such as the critic or wise person.

You will probably find that the figure once had a positive purpose but that this has changed over the years.

thought forms

Opening up intuitively can act like a beacon for some of the undesirable entities that people the realm close to earth. Learning how to dissolve such figures is strongly protective – and sensible.

Thought forms are, as the name suggests, created by the power of thought. Strong beliefs, emotions or fears may well create a thought form. They feed off desire, jealousy, envy and hatred, but they also feed off love. Such forms appear to be human – or demonic – and may well communicate in the guise of a 'real person'.

Recognizing thought forms

There are a great many thought forms hanging around. Some get strongly attached to a person, or a family. Others are what the Tibetans call 'hungry ghosts', which are created from all the unsatisfied desires of humankind. They are easy to contact. The problem is, a thought form's knowledge is extremely limited. So any 'intuition' that comes from such a source is rarely useful.

When you have some experience of working intuitively, it is easy to recognize a thought form. Although it can appear powerful, it somehow lacks vitality and is inflexible. A most effective way to deal with a thought form is by saying firmly: 'I don't believe in you.' Laughter also dissolves them. You can always use the light wand from page 145.

CREATING PETER

It is possible to create a thought form. A few years ago, parapsychology researchers in Canada conducted an experiment. A group sat together in meditation and thought a 'communicator from the other side' into being. They gave him a detailed history and a name – Peter. Despite the fact that this was fictitious, a communicator called Peter was contacted through several mediums and gave the same history every time. The more often he communicated, the more certain he was that he was a real person. Eventually, the researchers had to think him out of existence.

Fear can easily create a thought form. Reading the wrong kind of books or watching certain films can attach what may appear to be a demonic entity to you. Knowing that it exists only in the mind is excellent protection.

CHAPTER eight

Body awareness

'My beliefs I test on my body, on my intuitional consciousness, and when I get a response there, then I accept.'

D. H. Lawrence

bodily intuition

*Your body, especially if you are kinaesthetic, is the source of
enormous intuitive guidance, which can be tapped into through muscle
testing or by learning to listen to your body.*

Body responses can be highly intuitive. If you have ever had a gut feeling, you have had an intuition via body awareness. If you have ever entered a room and the hairs on the back of your neck stood up, your body was intuitively reacting to an unseen presence or to danger. If you have ever held an object belonging to another person and had a shudder run through you or felt a frisson of excitement, you have had an instinctive body response.

The body, however, does more than read vibrations or react in an instinctive way. The body has what Ken Dychtwald christened the 'bodymind'. This is an awareness of its own which can communicate its intuitions directly through the body. To Dychtwald, the body is a highly intelligent, all-knowing system with far more potential than it is usually given credit for: 'I view the body-mind as the evolutionary storehouse for all of life's potentials.'

Harnessing bodily reactions

Dowsing is one of the fastest ways of tapping into your intuition. You can use tools such as rods or pendulums, but it is possible to dowse without any equipment at all. As with most metaphysical activities, no one quite knows how dowsing works. It has been suggested that the subconscious mind, which can move beyond space and time to access information not available to the conscious mind, 'twitches' muscles that suddenly jerk dowsing rods upward or sideways, or cause a pendulum to rotate.

It is hard to believe that a twitching muscle can create the complex star patterns that some pendulums trace, but it is possible to accept that the sub-conscious mind can control your fingers, holding them firm if the answer is yes but releasing them if the reply is negative. You can take advantage of this simple method of accessing guidance to all kinds of questions, including testing your food, vitamin supplements, flower remedies and such like to see if they will be beneficial for you or not.

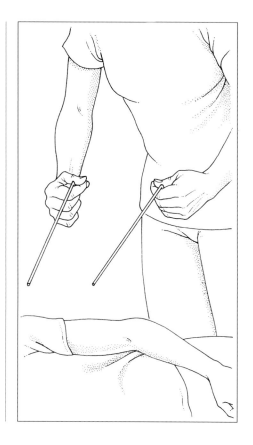

embodying intuition

Muscle testing can give extremely accurate intuitive information about your own body and its needs. You can also use this method to ask questions about your emotional issues.

Muscle testing is a useful way to access your body's intuition. If you are alone, finger dowsing can be suitable (see page 208). However, if you have a friend who can help you, you can considerably extend your access to your body's awareness. Muscle testing is particularly appropriate for health questions, but it can also be used for psychological and emotional matters. The success of muscle testing centres around the body having strength when the answer is 'yes' and the matter is good for you, and its lack of strength when the answer is 'no' and the matter detrimental.

To muscle test

- Stand upright with your feet slightly apart. Put one arm straight out sideways from the shoulder (if you are right-handed you will probably find it best to put out your right arm and if you are left-handed, your left arm).

- Ask your friend to stand behind you, with a hand on the wrist of your outstretched arm. When your friend says 'Resist' and pushes down on your arm (without undue pressure), try to keep it as firm as possible. You should be able to resist quite easily.

- Now put something in your other

hand that you suspect is bad for you (such as cigarettes, sugar, chocolate, a food to which you are allergic). Place that hand over and slightly above your heart. Your friend should once again say 'Resist' and push down on your wrist. Your arm will probably feel extremely weak as it drops to your side.

When to muscle test

This method can be used to test food allergies or to choose complementary remedies or supplements. You can also test how strong the organs of your body are by putting your hand on them and trying to resist a downward push on the outstretched arm.

If you want to know which parent had the strongest influence over you as a child, put your hand on your heart. Say 'mother' out loud and have your friend push down on your wrist. Then say 'father' and do the same. The parent associated with the weakest push down was the more dominant one. You can also test for chronic destructive emotions; place your hand over your heart, name the emotion and check the body's response.

Muscle testing is particularly appropriate for health questions, but it can be used for psychological and emotional matters.

finger dowsing

Finger dowsing is an extremely fast and accurate way to check the answer to questions which can be answered with a simple 'yes' or 'no'. It answers immediately and unambiguously.

There is nothing magical about finger dowsing – although it often looks like magic. The power of intuition to hold your thumb and finger together for a 'yes' answer and to let them part for a 'no' has no logical explanation. But you can replicate the action time and time again.

Finger dowsing is a reliable method of contacting your intuition. It is an excellent way to check a course of action and to guide your day-to-day life. If you are left-handed, follow the instructions on the opposite page. If the results are a little ambiguous, switch hands and link the left thumb and finger, as the intuitive connection may be stronger. As with all things intuitive, you must believe that you can succeed, so hold a strong intention that your hands will respond.

'What we achieve inwardly will change outer reality.' Otto Bank

TO FINGER DOWSE

- Hold the thumb and finger of your right hand together to form a loop (see diagram opposite). Now interlock the thumb and finger of your left hand through the loop to make a chain.

- Ask your question clearly, precisely and unambiguously. It must be phrased in such a way that it will have a straight 'yes' or 'no' answer. It does not have to be spoken aloud, although it can be, but you must concentrate and your mind must be focused as you ask the question.

- Try to pull your hands apart. If you cannot pull them apart, the answer is yes. If they part, the answer is no.

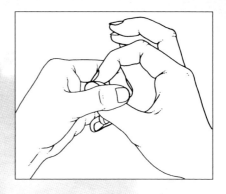

Thumbcheck

When you become competent at this form of finger dowsing, try varying it. With the thumb and finger of the hand you write with, hold your other thumb below the knuckle and pull as you ask your question. If it holds, the answer is yes, if it pulls off, the answer is no. Use whichever suits you best.

dowsing rods

Using dowsing rods is a very ancient skill but one which, it is estimated, 80 per cent of people can easily learn. Traditionally, dowsers were often known as 'water witches'.

Dowsing rods were traditionally made of hazel wood. A Y-shape would be cut from the hedgerow and used to find underground water. Some dowsers were so accurate in their dowsing that they could specify exactly how many feet into the ground a well shaft would have to go before it struck water. Dowsing rods can also be used to locate pipes and cables, to find minerals and ley lines, or to seek buried treasure.

As with all intuitive processes, you can train yourself to listen to your inner knowing while dowsing. Initially, you will probably find that the rods twitch, but you are not aware of why. With practice, you will begin to recognize the signals that water, electricity, caves and so on give off.

Initially, you will probably find that the rods twitch, but you are not aware of why.

You could use traditional hazel for your dowsing rods. If so, choose a piece with a diameter about the same as your little finger. You will need a branch that splits into an equal V-shape. Cut it about two to three hands' span above and below the V. Hold the rod at waist height with one hand on each of the branches and the bottom part of the Y straight out in front of you. When you reach your objective, the rod will make a distinctive twitch in your hands.

Making dowsing rods

You can purchase metal dowsing rods or make a pair from a wire coat hanger. Cut the hook off the coat hanger and cut the remaining wire into two equal pieces. Hold one piece loosely in each hand. As you walk forward, the rods will cross or move backward and forward as you reach a pipe and so on.

PRACTISING DOWSING

Practise at a place where you know there is a water pipe or drain. You need to be specific. If you say 'Show me water', the rods will show you water whether it is in a small pipe or a huge underground spring, and may twitch at other energies. Distinguishing which is which will come with practice. Walk slowly forward, holding your rods. When you feel a strong reaction, stop and mark the spot. Then walk forward again. The rods will move again when you get to the other side so that you can establish the width. Then turn round and walk back, again marking the spots where the rods react. Check whether the two edges coincide. If so, you have probably found your pipe.

pendulum dowsing

Pendulum dowsing is extremely easy to master and is an excellent tool for extending your intuition and your body's response to the world. While you can buy special crystal pendants, even a key hung from a string will be effective.

Using a pendulum is an excellent way to locate lost objects, to ask advice from your inner guidance, to check out information and to answer virtually any yes/no or timing question. If you want to establish food allergies or choose remedies or essential oils you can list the possibilities, run your finger down, and stop at the one that says yes. You can also use this method to make other choices.

You need to be strongly focused and to phrase your question correctly. If not, the pendulum will return to neutral or the energy will go out of the swing. Before starting a dowsing session, it is usual to check if it is right to dowse and ask that the dowsing be for the highest good of all concerned.

Clear intent

Clarity of intention, focus and trust are essential for good dowsing. The answer may not yet be settled, in which case the pendulum will reflect the uncertainty. An unclear response often indicates that you are not asking quite the right question. You need to be precise and avoid ambiguity. Having asked your question, do not keep checking. Trust.

You can use a purpose-made pendulum of wood, metal or stone, but if you do not have a pendulum, any suitable object on a chain or cord can be used – wedding rings on cotton were traditionally used to determine the sex of an unborn child.

Mastering the pendulum

Hold the pendulum between your thumb and forefinger with about a hand's breadth of chain hanging down. Wrap the spare chain around your fingers so that it does not get in the way. Begin by programming in 'yes' and 'no'. Set the pendulum moving backward and forward in a straight line. Tell yourself this is 'no'. Then set the pendulum swinging in another direction. Tell yourself this is 'yes'.

If the pendulum stops or wobbles, the answer will be 'maybe', or it could indicate that it is an inappropriate question to ask or not the time to be asking.

Timing

Pendulums can be used to ask 'when' questions. They can establish dates and ages. Draw a half moon on a piece of paper. Mark 0 at one end and 10 at the other. Hold the pendulum at the centre of the half moon. The pendulum will swing toward the correct number. If you want to

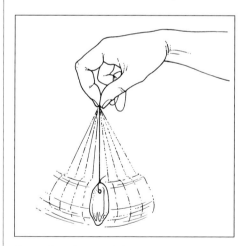

Mastering the pendulum

work with numbers higher than ten, ask the pendulum if it is greater than 10, 20, 30 etc. Use the half-moon numbers to refine the answer.

Map dowsing

Hold the pendulum over a map or plan and move it around slowly in a grid. This can be used to locate lost objects, to find a good place for a holiday or to choose a new area to live.

To be successful at dowsing, you must hold a clear intent and a strong picture in your mind of what you want to know. The stronger the 'yes' swing, the more emphatic the answer.

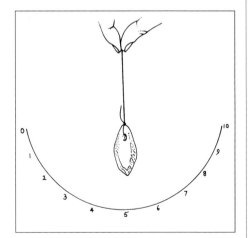

Timing

Map dowsing

use your pendulum

You can use a pendulum in many different situations – to choose food supplements, to recover missing objects, and to make decisions. Whatever you ask, make your question clear and unambiguous.

- **Find**
  Lost objects
  Missing people or pets
  Unknown information
  Underground water
  Buried treasure
  Minerals
  Oil
  Electric cables

- **Choose the right**
  Minerals and vitamins
  Remedy/medicine
  Food or diet
  Place to live

  Holiday destination
  School
  Career
  Car
  Therapist or teacher

- **Check**
  Potential for success
  Allergies
  Course of action
  Doubtful situations
  Someone's integrity
  Whether to go ahead
  Compatibility with
  partners, friends,

  employers
  Food suitability
  Water purity
  Chakra functioning

- **Make**
  Good business and
  personal decisions
  Consumer choices
  Career moves
  Health diagnoses

- **Answer**
  Yes/no or timing
  questions

'The first point of wisdom is to discern what is false; the second is to determine what is true.'

Lactantius

what do my hands tell me?

Your fingers and palms have great sensitivity, which can be further developed with a little practice. They can be used for intuitive massage or to read messages from everyday items.

As you develop intuitive skills, you will find your hands know exactly where to go during a massage without your rational mind intervening. Such massage is excellent for taking the aches and pains out of your partner's back or for soothing children. However, the hands' sensitivity can be used to learn more about other people. Psychometry picks up impressions from objects that belong to others.

Receiving impressions

As with so much else in the intuitive world, the first step is to recognize how you receive the impressions. They may come at a feeling level – you may feel very sad or joyful. You may shake with fear or apprehension or bubble with anticipation. You may find you see pictures or hear a voice telling you about the owner. You may have to trust yourself and start talking, and you will probably be as surprised as the owner of the object at what comes out of your mouth. Most people are adept at hiding their deepest feelings, so even if the object belongs to someone you know well, you can still be surprised at how they feel or what secrets they hide behind the façade.

EXERCISE

TO PRACTISE PSYCHOMETRY

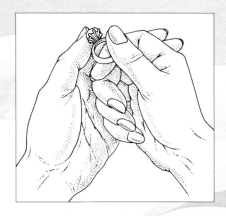

- Sit quietly, holding the object in your hand, with your hands comfortably in your lap. Breathe deeply and exhale slowly. Do this three times. Drop your shoulders. Do not strain to make things happen.
- Take your time, gently opening yourself up to the impressions that you receive. Notice how you are feeling. Has this changed since you picked up the object? What thoughts go through your mind?
- Share what you perceive with the owner of the object. Do not try to interpret, just tell them exactly the impressions you received, no matter how silly they may seem.

Feedback is extremely useful when you are practising, so be sure that you choose someone who will wholeheartedly share with you how accurate your impressions have been. Continue to hold the object as they talk, as you may well get more impressions along the way.

body talk

Your body will have been trying to communicate with you intuitively all your life. Most people unconsciously react when they hear a lie. This innate ability can be made conscious.

Most people are familiar with the notion of body language: the unconscious stance that says so much about how a person feels. If you observe someone hunched up, covering their solar plexus with one hand and an ear with the other, not only are they not liking what they are hearing but they are also none too happy about the vibes that person is giving off. Body talk goes deeper than this.

Many people unconsciously grimace or twitch when they hear a lie or something that does not ring true for them. A pain in the neck can indicate someone around who is exactly that. If you can bring these unconscious reactions to your attention, you can tune into your body's intuitions and learn to recognize its subtle signals. To do so successfully, you will need the help of an observant and perceptive friend.

EXERCISE
Body reaction appraisal

- Prepare in advance a list of statements, some of which you strongly agree with, others with which you strongly disagree; some of which are lies, some of which are the truth. Include several 'yes' or 'no' questions to which you will not give a verbal answer but will think the reply in your mind.

- First you, and then your friend, will read out your list.
- Ask your friend to monitor closely your body's reactions, paying attention to such things as jerks, rumblings, grimaces and twitches.
- Small signals will be important. For instance, the left index finger could twitch for yes and the right for no.
- Once you have your friend's observations, repeat the exercise, trying to be aware yourself of your body's responses.

Expanding body awareness

Develop the habit of paying attention to what your body is telling you at all times. The major areas of intuitive response, beyond finger twitches and the like, are in your gut and solar plexus.

Next time you are in the middle of a conversation, suddenly stop paying attention to what is being said. Half close your eyes and let them go out of focus. Bring your attention into your body and see what it senses is going on, taking your mind down to your solar plexus and gut. After a while, this becomes automatic and you will act on intuitions received in this way without thinking about it.

A pain in the neck can indicate someone around who is exactly that.

CHAPTER nine

Your sixth sense

'Our minds have the most remarkable ability to provide those resources that we most need at any given time.'

David Michie

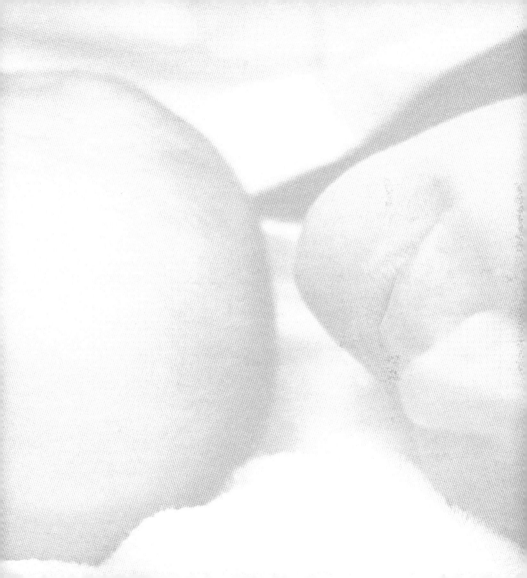

furthering your intuition

*By this stage of the course, if you have completed all the
exercises, your intuition will be tuned up and working very well.
The more you use it, the better it will function.*

Use it or lose it. It is a question of building on your strengths, putting the knowledge you have about how your intuition functions into practice, paying even more attention to signals, and trying out new ways of stimulating your innate ability.

Catching the signals

Meditate under the observation of a perceptive partner who is aware of your body response to intuition (see page 220). Every time they see a signal, they should ask: 'What was your awareness just then?' This teaches you to catch the fleeting insights that pass through. Asking 'How did you feel just then?' might elicit a different kind of answer, one from your emotional intuition. Take up the habit of monitoring yourself.

Telepathy

Telepathy games can be played at an agreed time each day or in a spare moment. For this you need a partner, present or at a distance, and a pack of coloured or Zener cards. Decide in advance who will be sender and who will receive (you can change over after an agreed time). The sender should shuffle the cards and turn them face up one at a time (without the receiver seeing them). Concentrate on sending the colour or the symbol to your partner. Fill your mind with it to the exclusion of all else. The receiver sits with a quiet, receptive mind and writes down whatever floats into his or her mind. Then change around. At the end of the time, compare notes and check the scores.

As your telepathic ability strengthens, try sending your partner messages not only at pre-arranged times, but also intermittently at any odd moment. Remember to be receptive to any message your partner might send you.

Clairvoyance

Clairvoyance can be used to tune into guidance from discarnate entities or to read the contents of sealed envelopes and so on. Although it is called 'sight', not all clairvoyants 'see'. Many feel or know the messages they receive. To develop reliable clairvoyance fully, you need to be under the mentorship of someone who has clear sight and who can discern who is trying to communicate with you until you have this ability yourself. Not every communicator has good intentions or is necessarily truthful. A mentor can also aid in recognizing whether what you

'In the heart of every human being lies the flower of intuition.

Alice Bailey

'see' is symbolic or actual, and how to present the information.

If you do find that you are receiving 'messages', check with your guardian that they are coming to you in truth and light before you proceed. Try to describe the person who is giving you the message but don't worry at this stage if you get details like hair or eye colour wrong – it will become clearer. Check who the message is for and be clear as to content. Record the experience in your journal.

Practise reading the contents of sealed envelopes or unopened books. This can be a useful technique. In the thesis for my university degree I quoted from a book with relevant research that confirmed a theory I was proposing, but did not reference its date. I could not lay my hands on the book again and when I consulted the library catalogue, I could find no trace. Two years later, browsing in a book shop, I came across it. It had recently been published for the first time. When I met the author, I found that she completed the manuscript at the time I wrote my thesis. I had plucked it out of the ether. The page number and publisher were correct, though these had not been decided then.

Initially, practise on actual books or correspondence, unopened in front of you.

EXERCISE
Reading a sealed envelope
Sit down quietly, relax, breathe gently and bring your attention to the envelope in your hands. Picture yourself opening the envelope, unfolding the letter, spreading it out and reading it. If you cannot get it word for word, try to absorb the sense of it. Then open the actual letter and see how you did.

You can adapt the above to 'read' a book. Decide in advance which page you are going to 'open' it to, and picture yourself doing this and reading it.

Clairaudience

Many people who are clairaudient 'hear' at a point behind and slightly to the left or right of them rather than through physical ears, but they may tune into an inner ear. Develop the habit of lightly listening while you are in a meditative or relaxed state – concentrating heavily is counterproductive. Initially it is rather like tuning in a radio with a lot of static and crackle. Picture a dial tuning it in more clearly.

Channelling

Channelling is best taught under personal supervision as an enormous amount of rubbish can come through – some of it is part of the process, some of it is deliberate misguidance. Most people who channel have no idea what will come out of their mouth until they say it, so it takes courage to open your mouth and allow. If you are going to do this, you need an empathetic audience to help. As with clairvoyance, it is better initially to have someone who is aware of who, or what, is communicating. If you find yourself channelling, try to record what is said and assess the result carefully. To avoid unwanted channelling, close your crown chakras tightly.

Inner wisdom

Accessing your own inner wisdom becomes easier the more you meditate. Sit quietly and ask specific questions, or allow a stream of wisdom to rise up in your awareness. As this can easily be forgotten, record it at the time.

Automatic writing

There are two forms of automatic writing. One is totally automatic. You simply hold a pen loosely in your hand (the modern equivalent is to turn on your computer) and allow it to move by itself. The other is to write down everything that passes through your mind. If you are a proficient typist, you can allow your hands to type without your thinking processes being involved. Initially the everyday mind tends to want to censor. If your mind insists on interfering, keep it occupied with a task such as counting backward in threes from a hundred down to one.

Further body awareness

If you let it, your body can be naturally intuitive. Getting up when someone is approaching out of sight is natural for the body – it is an ancient defence mechanism. This can work for you if you allow it to. While you are waiting for someone, tell yourself that you will step forward the minute they get to a certain point out of your sight line. Then allow your body to do this. Eventually you will never need to hang around waiting for anyone; you will instinctively know the right moment to arrive because your body will be in tune with the person you are meeting.

This ability of the body to know when someone draws near is useful if you have to walk unaccompanied in dark places. You can send your intuition ahead to check out the energy of the place and to help you to keep safe.

If you have to pass anyone about whom you feel uneasy, an ancient occult technique is to cloak your light so that you will not be noticed. As soon as you become aware of the person approaching, ask your guardian: 'Make my light dim, make me invisible.' Remember to become visible again later.

emotional intuition

Just as the emotions and feelings you experience can affect your intuitive ability at any given time, so too can intuition operate at a feeling and emotional level that centres around the heart.

Intuition is not just a matter for the mind. It belongs to the emotions too. As psychotherapist and mythographer Jean Shinoda Bolen explains: 'To know how to choose a path with heart is to learn how to follow intuitive feeling. Logic can tell you superficially where a path might lead to, but it cannot judge whether your heart will be in it.'

Your emotions tell you how you intuitively feel about something. The sites of your emotions are the solar plexus, the higher heart chakra and the heart. You can recognize the part the emotional self plays in intuition and the intelligence with which your emotions can guide you once they become conscious. If they remain at the level of wishful thinking or

'The heart has its reasons which reason knows nothing of.' Blaise Pascale

subconscious traps, they lead to suspect intuition. Most people have emotional triggers and needs that they are unaware of. Knowing what is going on in your emotional centre is a powerful way of enhancing your intuition. Automatically tuning in to what is going on in your heart and solar plexus, and the feelings that you have about things and people, helps you to be more emotionally intelligent as well as intuitive. It can save a lot of heartbreak, too.

EXERCISE
Enhancing emotional intuition

Stop whatever you are doing. Close your eyes and take your attention into your heart. How does it feel? Is it joyful and expectant? Or is it heavy and dull? Let your heart speak to you.

Now take your attention down to your solar plexus. How does this feel? Is it calm and peaceful or churning and uneasy? Are you harbouring destructive emotions such as guilt or anger? If so, let them dissolve or resolve to do something constructive with them.

If uneasy, check out which emotional buttons have been pressed. Look at the events that created those buttons, forgive anyone involved, and let them go. Switch the button to 'off', permanently. If your frustrated hopes and wishes are involved, check out whether they are still appropriate. If not, let them go.

Now check out how you feel about things. Are you happy with the situation around you, the people you are in contact with? Is there anything you can do to improve things? Ask your emotional intuition to speak to you.

Then bring your attention back to the present moment and put the insights you have gained into practice.

intuition and creativity

Intuitives see the world in a wider way. The more intuitive you are, the more creative energy you will have available and the greater the insights you will be able to draw into your creative expression.

'It should not be hard for you to stop sometimes and look into the stains of walls, or ashes of a fire, or clouds, or mud, or like places in which you may find really marvellous ideas.'

Leonardo da Vinci, *Notebooks*

There is an enormous amount of evidence, mostly anecdotal and experiential but nonetheless indisputable, that creativity is an intuitive process. Great thinkers, artists and scientists have relied on intuition throughout the ages:

> *'[The pioneer scientist must have] a vivid intuitive imagination for new ideas are not generated by deduction, but by artistically creative imagination.'*
> Max Planck

> *'You have only to work up imagination to the state of vision and the thing is done.'*
> William Blake

Intuition and creativity go hand in hand. As artist David Whyte explains: 'You feed your longing and desires and they do the work. My whole life has been following my intuition and strange beckonings.' Artists and inventors have learned to pay attention to the elusive thought, the inspiration that slips unseen from other minds. Niels Bohr, the atomic physicist, confessed that he had not worked out his complex atomic models by classical mechanics but rather by intuition. He dreamt he was on a giant gas sun around which planets whirled, whistling as they passed, each attached to the sun by a filament. The dream represented events within the atom. As Ralph Waldo Emerson perceptively said: 'In every work of genius we recognize our own rejected thoughts.'

As Einstein pointed out: 'The formulation of a problem is often more essential than its solution, which may be merely a matter of mathematical or experimental skill. To raise new questions, new possibilities, to regard old questions from a new angle, requires creative imagination and marks real advances in science.'

overcoming creative blocks

Intuition often points the way to new creativity but almost everyone occasionally experiences a creative block. Fortunately, the power of the mind soon dissolves this and shows the way forward.

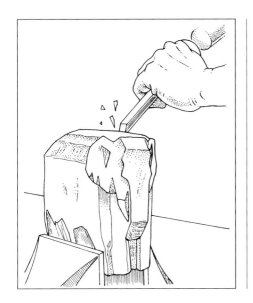

A sculptor was asked how he created a statue of an elephant from a block of stone. He answered: 'I chip away everything that is not elephant.' He was able to discern the form of the elephant within the stone and reveal it.

Everyday creativity

Many people find themselves confronted with creative blocks and you don't have to be a great artist or writer to create. Decorating your home, landscaping your garden or making a delicious meal are creative acts. So too is living your life to the full. Making the most of your talents and potential is creative. If you feel blocked in any area of your life, the following simple exercise can reveal the way forward.

EXERCISE
Creativity exercise

- Seat yourself comfortably and take yourself into your favourite place (see page 128). Spend a few moments enjoying this beautiful space. Engage all your senses to really feel it, smell it and see it.
- Then, if you walk a little way to one side, you will find that a large block of stone or a hunk of wood has been left for you, along with a mallet, chisels and smoothing materials.
- Walk around your block. Look at it from all sides. Feel its texture, its warmth or coolness. Allow an image of what this block might hold to come into your mind.

- Pick up the tools, weigh them in your hand. See how each one is specially shaped for the task it performs.
- Using these tools, allow your hands to begin chipping away at the block to reveal the image at its centre. Hear the sound of the hammer, feel the flakes as they chip off. Look at how the colour changes. If you are working on wood, it will release its own special smell.
- When your image is revealed, use the smoothing and polishing materials to bring out its full beauty.
- When it is complete, make your way back to the centre of your favourite place. Think about your creation. What did it mean to you? What did it signify? How did you feel about it?
- Then bring your attention back into the room and write up your experience in your Intuition Journal.

CHAPTER ten

Intuition in action

'We know more than
we know we know.'

Michael Polanyi

living intuitively

*When you live in harmony with your intuition, it becomes
something that is not apart from your daily life – it underpins it. If you
allow it to, it will transform your life.*

Coming from a place of intuitive trust totally changes your approach. You no longer need be defensive, aggressive, suspicious or self-orientated. You can be open with people and allow your life to flow effortlessly. This is not a passive process, however. It is dynamic. You need to be attentive, fully present and aware, and you also need to act when appropriate. Following intuitive guidance, you will instinctively know what is needed, the actions to take, the decisions to make. You will be in the right place at the right time. People will be drawn into your orbit to facilitate your path. The right job will come along or the old one will open out. Life becomes harmonious, your well-being is enhanced, your abundance assured.

Effortless flow

A life that runs smoothly is far less stress-ful and much more is achieved with far less effort expended. Before you begin a project, make a phone call, or start a conversation with someone, take a moment to tune in. Check that you are on the right path, that this action is beneficial (using the finger pull can be helpful here until knowing becomes instantaneous, see page 209). Empathizing at an intuitive level makes contact far easier and deeper and creates a cooperative atmosphere. If you have to point something out, or complain, for instance, take the time to rehearse mentally. See yourself making your point and it being received and dealt with constructively. Visualize a successful outcome to anything and it will manifest in your life.

If you want to make contact with someone but don't know where they are, send a message out into the ether. When I urgently needed my housesitter and he was uncontactable by phone, I pictured him, told him the day I needed to leave, and mentally asked him to arrive in time. He walked in with an hour to spare. But I knew he would be there as we had a strong intuitive connection. I use this same principle to find a parking space, to get to the train or airport at exactly the right time, and to attract the particular person I need to make contact with in a big gathering – whether I am aware of their identity or not. I allow myself to be in a receptive space that draws to me what

Following intuitive guidance, you will instinctively know what is needed, the actions to take, the decisions to make.

I need. Note that I say what I 'need' rather than what I would 'like'. I have found that what I think I would like is not always what I really need. Sometimes this brings apparent difficulties, delays or sidetracks into my life. Trusting that this is still right can be difficult, but it inevitably proves to be so, although sometimes my intuition works without telling me what is going on! Holding trust and the right intention is absolutely essential.

Living intuitively can even save your life. Perceiving that a car is coming moments before it comes round the corner on the wrong side of the road can avoid accidents, as can instinctively recognizing

EVERYDAY CLUES

The everyday world is full of clues as to what you should – or should not – be doing. Learning to pay attention to these makes your life flow much more smoothly. If, for instance, you are trying to book a hotel for a weekend away and the system is down or the phone continuously engaged, stop and ask the question: 'Is this what would be most beneficial – or appropriate – for me at this time?' In one such case, where someone went ahead without asking the question, illness prevented the planned trip at the last moment and the cost of the hotel was lost. Conversely, when the signal was noted and a trip postponed, a damaged tyre and an exhaust dropping off the car while close to home made it clear why a long journey would have been unwise.

that a car is about to pull out in front of you or that someone is going to brake suddenly. Use the finger-pull or thumb-check method of dowsing to confirm if it is safe to pull out when you are at a place with a restricted view.

Finding a parking place

It is possible to send your intuition ahead of you to spot a parking place, automatically guiding you in the right direction. But you can go further than this. Your intuition can create that parking spot. Picture an empty space waiting for you exactly where you need it. Trust the picture, and there it will be.

Instant access

While you can use your intuition to tell you when someone is available, you can also use it to ensure that they are there when you need them. Take a few

moments to bring your attention into yourself. Picture the person you want to speak to, whether in person or by telephone, and picture them available, helpful and ready to give you their full attention and cooperation. They will soon be available in actuality.

problem solving

Allowing your intuition to solve problems makes life flow more smoothly. If you have a problem to which you cannot find a solution, the exercise will provide an effective answer.

- Spend a few minutes writing out your problem – list the ways you have tried to solve it, the difficulties you have had and the blocks you have come up against. Be as specific and detailed as possible, but avoid excuses.
- Put your pen away and close your eyes.
- Breathe gently and easily. Now think about your problem and why you would like to find a solution. Be as succinct and positive as possible.
- Take your attention away from your problem and leave it in the hands of your intuition. Meanwhile,

take yourself to your favourite place (see page 128). Explore it, see the sights, hear the sounds, and smell its perfumes. Take as long as you like.

- Then, when you are ready, look around. You will see a building away to one side. Make your way over there, feeling the ground beneath your feet and the pull of your muscles as you walk.

- When you reach the building, stand by the door. Put out your hand and touch the door. Feels its texture beneath your fingers. Notice how it feels. Then find the door handle. Open it, and go inside. There you will find the solution to your problem.

- Remember to ask how you will implement the solution to bring about an optimum result.

- When you have learnt all you need,

come back through the door, bringing the solution with you. Make your way back to your favourite place and return your attention into the room.

- Write down your solution, and how you will implement, it as fully as possible, making sure you use the present tense.

- At least once a day, read aloud your solution. Be sure to put in motion any action required. Your intuition can show you how to solve a problem, but it needs action on your part to manifest an outcome.

- Pin up your solution where you will be sure to see it every day – for example, over the washbasin or on the fridge door. This way your subconscious will cooperate with you in bringing the solution into concrete manifestation.

the art of object placement

Feng shui is the Ancient Chinese art that enhances the environment, especially within the home but also in the workplace. Your intuition can similarly place objects for optimum energy flow.

Having the objects and pictures in your home or office in a harmonious placement helps the flow of energy and enhances your environment. Your intuition can be used to help you find the perfect placement of crystals, furniture and objects. While you will need to discover your own unique signal, many people find that the hairs on the back of their arms stand up when the placement is exactly right. Other people get a shudder down their back or their feet tingle.

If you are unsure whether you have found exactly the right place, leave the object in place or a picture on the wall for 24 hours and check out how you feel about it. You will intuitively know when it is right.

Other people get a shudder down their back or their feet tingle.

THE ARTFUL ASSISTANT

An intuitive Feng Shui practitioner was called to the house of a tarot reader. The tarot reader's work was successful, but something was missing. She was not quite as sharp as she knew she could be. As soon as the practitioner walked into the kitchen, her attention was pulled to a striking photograph of a woman. The woman's nose was pointing toward the back door, sending her energy out of the house. The practitioner learned that this was her client's mother. She instinctively felt that this woman was trying to help with the tarot readings, but was prevented from making full contact because her photograph was in the wrong place. It was moved into the tarot reader's work room. Both the practitioner and the reader immediately felt a huge surge of energy. The tarot readings were spot on.

In another consultation, the practitioner realized that two portraits had their backs to each other, metaphorically speaking. This was particularly significant because they were placed in the relationship corner of the room. She moved them to face each other. The hairs on the back of her arms stood straight up and the energy in the room changed completely. Within weeks, the relationship had taken a dramatic turn for the better. The practitioner commented that these signals were invaluable in her work. She knew just by looking at something whether or not its placement was beneficial. If she got a buzz, it was. If not, she moved it until the energy changed.

intuition and healing

*Some intuitives merely have to look at someone to diagnose an
internal illness or emotional dis-ease. While ability at this level is rare,
it is easy to develop your healing intuition.*

If you regularly scan your body, and
check your emotional equilibrium,
you can help maintain health and
increase your sense of well-being.

EXERCISE
The body scan

- Sit down comfortably, close your eyes,
relax and breathe easily. Take your
attention to the top of your head and
down to your sinus passages. Check that
they are unobstructed. Then move to
your eyes. Check out how they feel and
how they are functioning. Do the same
for your ears. Notice if anything feels

out of balance, and place healing light
there if needed.

- Begin to move your attention down
through your brain. Check out each part
as you come to it, including the
pituitary and pineal glands. Make sure
the blood and chemical mix is flowing
well, the neural connections are all firing
in sequence, and the endocrine system is
properly regulated. If any part is blocked
or malfunctioning, picture healing light
flowing through it.

- Move your attention into your neck and
shoulders, checking out your thyroid
gland and voice box (if your thyroid

'Here in this body
are the sacred rivers:
here are the sun and
moon as well as all the
pilgrimage places.
I haven't encountered
another temple as blissful
as my own body.'

feels 'fast' or 'slow', picture the control mechanism as a scale and bring the pointer back to normal), and down your arms to your fingertips and back up again. Bathe any areas of stiffness in light. Bring your awareness down through your body, checking out each organ in turn and putting in healing light where necessary. Look at your lungs, thymus gland and heart. Then check out your oesophagus, stomach, liver and pancreas. Follow your intestinal system through to its end. Return your attention to the spleen, kidneys and bladder and into the reproductive organs. Check that the organs of elimination are removing toxins efficiently and put in a 'cleaning team' to help if they are not.

- Take your attention to the blood circulating through your body. Check the arteries and veins that carry it, clearing any blockages with light.

- Now take your attention to your lymphatic system. Let your mind follow its channels, making sure that the lymph is flowing freely. Clear any blockages.
- Let your attention go on down through your thighs, knees and into your feet, checking as you go.
- Take your attention back to the top of your head. Picture a shaft of light coming down to envelop and pass through your body. Let a feeling of well-being flow through your whole body, energizing and healing as it goes.
- If you become aware of any area that does not return to balance and good health, be sure to check it out with your physician.
- By taking your attention into your solar plexus, you can check out your emotional health and dowse for appropriate flower essences to gently release and rebalance your emotions.

Biofeedback

Biofeedback uses the power of the mind to affect the body. Machines are often used, but your intuition is equally effectively.

EXERCISES
Regulating blood pressure

First establish the optimum blood pressure for a person your age. Close your eyes, and breathe gently. Feel your heart pumping your blood; sense its pressure and pulse. Tell your body to reset your blood pressure to the optimum. Feel it lowering until it reaches the perfect pressure. Instruct your body to keep it at optimum level.

Migraine or headache

Practice this exercise so that you can use it when necessary. At the first sign of a migraine, sit down, close your eyes, relax and breathe gently. Feel the palms of your hands become hotter and hotter.

Then take your attention to the back of your neck and feel it getting cooler and cooler. As the nape of your neck cools down, overdilation of the blood vessels ceases. Any prospective pain flows away.

Tell your body that whenever that first signal makes itself felt, your body will automatically make your hands hot and the nape of your neck cold. The migraine will be over before it has begun. (If muscle tension causes your headaches, tell your muscles to relax.)

Thyroid

To balance an under- or over-active thyroid, close your eyes and picture a scale from −10 to +10 with a moving pointer. Move the pointer to the optimum position for you. Instruct your body to keep it there and regulate the thyroid. (This exercise can be adapted for the immune system etc.)

intuition at work

Using your intuition can sharpen up your working day, help you find creative solutions to problems, encourage you to use your time more efficiently and improve your relationships with colleagues.

Once you are in the flow of using your intuition at work, the day-to-day struggle falls away, leaving far more time to be creative and fulfilled in your work.

- You act with total appropriateness. Freed from knee-jerk reactions, you find creative responses to pressing problems and chronic difficulties.
- You are intuitively aware of what is required from you in advance of it happening and therefore are more prepared and open to possible options and solutions.

- You are more creative in all aspects of your working life.
- You are able to 'think on your feet', dealing efficiently, quickly and spontaneously with whatever situation comes your way.
- You use your intuition to create contacts, setting up an intention in advance.
- You do not waste time trying to contact someone who is out. Your intuition tells you when they return and suggests positive steps to take in the meantime.
- Rehearsing the outcome you

want, through visualization, prepares the way to easy acceptance of plans and suggestions. It revolutionizes both sales techniques and people management.

- We are taught to rely on experts. Trusting to your own perceptions gets the job done far more efficiently and innovatively.
- Problems are exacerbated by what we think we know – knowledge, preconceptions and expectations get in the way. When you change to what is actually perceived, there are far fewer misunderstandings. Communication is clear and action brisk.
- You find new ways of looking at things. Henry Ford asked the question: 'How can we get the work to the people?', and the assembly line was born.

- You understand your fellow workers more acutely and your people skills improve. You are aware when someone's mood or energy is low or high – and act accordingly. Taking time for an empathetic word revolutionizes relationships with colleagues.
- You think the unthinkable and do the impossible – and take the necessary risks to achieve that.
- Group skills become more cooperative and you find joy in teamwork.
- Empathetic and intuitive managers allow rather than trying to control the situation or other people. They are aware of problems and potentials before they occur, and take appropriate steps.
- You rise effortlessly to the top of your profession.

empathy at work

When speaking to a colleague you want to be more in tune with,
and communicate more effectively with, try holding the phone to your left
ear or cover your right ear with your hand.

There is evidence to suggest that the impulses received by the left ear go to the right brain, which is far more empathetic than the left. On the other hand, if you are in a business situation, for instance, and want to detach yourself and be more objective, put the telephone to your right ear.

Intuitive leadership
People who are strongly intuitive become leaders. They may not set out to do so, but people follow them instinctively, especially as their people skills and management style are empathetic and personally motivating rather than coercive and authoritarian. Other people respect an intuitive leader's

Intuitive people are 'inner led'. Listening to their inner voice, they do not need an outer authority to get them to act.

judgement, their creativity, appropriateness and integrity, and they honour their courage and risk-taking – what seems like a risk to non-intuitive people is the obvious solution for an intuitive person.

Intuitive people are 'inner led'. Listening to their inner voice, they do not need an outer authority to get them to act. They are fearless and sure without being arrogant. They have passion which they are not afraid to express. And yet they care about the people they lead, they show understanding. They communicate with regard to people's concerns and objectives as well as those of the organization.

Within an intuitively led organization, everyone benefits. Work becomes more meaningful. There is a unity of purpose and people are inspired to produce their best work.

Because intuitive people are connected into the whole, everyone looks out for, and appreciates, everyone else in the organization, giving a sense of community.

> *'Leadership is not an affair of the head. It's not something you do by thinking about it hard. You do it from the heart, and when your heart is in your business and your business is in your heart, when your heart is with your family or your community or the people who work there, you get extraordinary things done.'*
> James M. Kouzes

Intuitive organizations

Organizations that function intuitively are people-orientated and concerned with the environment. A huge shift is taking place throughout the business world. Roles and responsibilities are being re-evaluated within the global scheme of things rather than the global market. Ethics and integrity are becoming increasingly important as solutions to humanity's problems become more and more pressing. Intuitive organizations readily recognize the interconnectedness of all life and, like leavening in bread, their vision is spreading.

INTUITIVE ORGANIZATIONS

- Think globally
- Are people-centred
- Treat everyone as of equal value
- Are ethical
- Look for innovative solutions
- Capitalize on individual creativity for the benefit of the whole
- Are elastic – flexible and forward-looking
- Respond to and create change
- Create rather than react

Group creativity

In an intuitive organization, the sum of the parts is much greater than the sum of individual members as group energy is heightened and enhanced by intuitive teamwork. At the same time, individual input is stimulated.

Research suggests that the brainstorming sessions that became fashionable in organizations during the 1980s and 90s may not be as conducive to group creativity as was first thought. There is evidence that certain individuals within the group will be more than happy to offer their contributions – in order to be noticed and for their own glory, rather than for the good of the group – and other, more introverted people who dislike taking risks, and who fear the judgement of the group, will hold back. This situation can lead to deep lack of trust within the group. In addition, as one of the major factors in creative intuition is that, initially, the idea comes as a picture that has to be translated into words, an intuitive idea can be difficult to express fully immediately.

Creative anonymity

It may well be more conducive to hold anonymous creative sessions in which everyone makes their contribution from their computer terminal. This removes fear of group judgement and the cult of personality from the equation. One of the best ways for this to work is for the group to convene, intuitively rather than physically, at a fixed time and to spend 20 minutes in quiet contemplation, consciously linking to the group mind and intention. Images and half-formed ideas can be entered onto the computer so that the whole group can explore them while the group mind is united.

EXERCISE
Embracing difference

If you have difficulties with a colleague, the following exercise will help you.

- Sit quietly for a moment or two, bringing your attention deep into yourself. When you feel ready, allow your awareness to rise up to the highest possible level until you reach the point where all is one.

- From this place, look at your colleague. Identify what irks and irritates you, what you dislike, what makes it difficult for you to get on together. As all is one, you will see that this is merely an extension of the things that irk and irritate you about yourself. Thank your colleague for being a mirror for you and embrace these traits within yourself. They have a positive gift for you. Take the time to allow your intuition to tell

you what it is. When you know,
resolve to put it into practice.

- Now find within that oneness all the
positive aspects of yourself and your
colleague. Embrace these and resolve
to manifest them more strongly in
your own life and to recognize them
within your colleague.

- Feel how much love there is between
you in this place of oneness and
bring this sensation back with you as
you slowly return your awareness to
the everyday world.

EXERCISE
Building the group mind

A group that links together becomes far
more creative. One person should be
chosen from the group to lead the exercise, and the topic and goal decided in
advance by the group as a whole.

- Close your eyes and breathe gently.

Raising your eyes and looking up to
the point above and between your
eyebrows, picture a yellow ribbon
going from this point up toward the
ceiling, where it meets the ribbon of
everyone else in the room. This is
where the group mind is situated.
Picture a bright light shining at
this point and sending beams down
into each individual mind to link
them together.

- Now take your mind to the topic
you are addressing today. Think about
it, setting out its problems, its potential
and its possible solutions. Look at the
goals and how they can be achieved.
As you think, let the light take your
thoughts into the group mind.

- It would be useful to have an 'advisory
committee' to help you, so ask that
everyone who has expertise in this
field will mentally unite with you

and give their input. Be receptive to their advice as you listen to your inner voice and to the group mind.

• Allow 5–15 minutes of quiet reflection time.

• Take a moment or two to finish what you are doing and go over the various solutions that have occurred to you.

• Now take your mind up to the joining point of the ribbons and detach your ribbon, bringing it back into yourself with your own individual mind, but know that you can access the group mind whenever it is appropriate. When you are ready, open your eyes. Feel your feet firmly on the ground.

• Appoint a group scribe who can record what is said on a large white board. Go round the group sharing all the insights and solutions that arose for each person and use them as a springboard for a group discussion.

CHAPTER eleven

Group work

'The perception of
separateness of an individual
from other persons
(or from the universe)
is an illusion.'

Willis K. Harman, Professor of Engineering-Economic Systems,
Stanford University

group practice

Groups are powerfully affected by intuition, whether they are intending this or not. Group interaction opens psychic links between participants, which can be purposely enhanced.

Intuition can be enhanced through group practice – and intuition can strongly affect group interaction. Some groups come together specially to enhance their intuition, but all groups benefit from intuitive exercises. It raises creativity and opens the way to risk-taking.

There is more interaction between a group than is apparent at surface level. At a very deep level, our minds are one. At a more superficial level, however, group dynamics can be disharmonious. Groups operate at the lowest common denominator. In a group that comes together with a spiritual purpose, jealousy and dissent can be rife if the highest connection has not been made. (The exercise on page 256 can be amended to reach group consciousness rather than the group mind.)

'The place where we agreed to meet
The space between thoughts.' Julie Chimes

Groups interact at a subtle level and if someone does not trust a member of the group at gut level that group will not function well – and the lack of trust may well be an intuition that should be listened to.

Group trust

Group trust can be enhanced by a few moments of silence, focused thought, or meditation, before commencing the business of the group. Sitting together in silence for a few moments melds the group together and opens the way to trust and openness.

If you are taking part in a brain-storming session to generate ideas or solutions, you could focus on the thought 'solutions'. Develop this further with a meditation to create a space within the centre of the group that attracts solutions into it, which make themselves known with clarity and ease to the group. It is also possible to programme a crystal to help the group. Cathedral quartz works extremely well for this purpose as it absorbs the group's intention, and transmits it back as clear thought. It also links into the universal mind and so helps to focus intuitive solutions.

The overall energy can be lifted if one or two people within the group are able to hold a higher energy for the others. Such an upliftment occurs naturally when the group mind is harmonized. If the brainwaves of the group are synchronized, not only will intuition be enhanced but also the overall consciousness of the whole group will be raised.

Rhythmic breathing harmonizes group brainwaves. Breathe in for a count of 4, hold it for 3, and out for 5.

Group protection

When you work in a metaphysical group, protection is as important as when you work alone. If you feel uncomfortable with someone in the group, it may be that you need to protect yourself from their energies. This is especially so if they are angry or disruptive. It is not a matter of shutting them out. It is more a matter of not allowing them to disturb your serenity. If you hold your own space, crystallize the edges of your biomagnetic field, and put them into a loving energy, you may well find that their attitude will change for the better.

Resolving group issues

It may also be that you need to explore exactly what makes you feel uncomfortable – this can be done through group discussion or between the two of you, perhaps with a third person present

as mediator. Remember that unresolved issues between group members are not conducive to group harmony. However, it may be that your intuition is working well and the person about whom you feel doubtful does not have the welfare of the group at heart. If this is the case, paying attention to your intuition could well be a timely warning.

Setting up the space

The purple pyramid meditation on page 131 is excellent for setting up a group space. The colour of the pyramid can vary in accordance with the purpose of the group. The pyramid could be set up by the group leader before the group assembles, but it will work much better if the whole group is involved in creating the safe space. Adding in some extra steps after bringing amethyst light down into the pyramid greatly enhances group cohesion.

- Feel the light activating the crown of your head. You will feel this open up. From your crown, your own light will shine. It will go up in a beam to the apex of the pyramid to join the light of all others in the group.
- This is the point where you all meet to become one mind. Your joint light goes up from the pyramid to meet the universal mind from which you can draw inspiration and intuition.
- When the group is ready to disband, disconnect all the beams of light, close the pyramid down and send its healing energies out to the world, wherever they are needed.
- As a symbol of the safe space you have created, you may like to place a piece of hematite in the centre of the group. Hematite enhances group trust, keeps it grounded and focused, and helps to maintain a safe space.

Closing the group

It is essential that the group is closed down properly and that people do not allow their energy to go home with anyone else or take anyone else's with them. A few words to close the group are useful, reminding people to pull their biomagnetic fields in around themselves, releasing any energy that is not theirs and letting it go back to where it belongs, and taking back any of their own energy from anyone else to whom it has gone. Some groups like to send out the energy that they have generated to wherever it is needed in the world for healing or any other purpose that is appropriate.

Before you leave a group, take your attention to where the energies meet. Detach your energy and bring back all that is yours; leave nothing behind. Check that the edges of your biomagnetic sheath are protecting you and close your chakras.

Group exercises

Exercises quickly bring a group together and open up intuition. Decide who will lead the group. The group should sit in a circle, preferably within arms' reach but having some space round each person. The leader has the task of speaking the preliminary instructions, setting the exercise in motion and closing the exercise. When the group leader is well attuned to the group, he or she will know how long the pauses should be and when to commence leading once more – and when to encourage gently a group participant who may lack confidence to speak out.

What colour am I?

The leader starts off by explaining to the group what will happen. First of all, they will be attuning to their own colour. Then they will look at the colours of the group.

THE BENEFITS OF SOUND

Sound is a useful harmonizer of group energy, bringing the group's brainwaves into alignment. Some groups use chanting – such as Om – while others find focusing on the sound of a Tibetan bowl, cymbals or a bell helpful. Monks and nuns used plainsong to induce a meditative state.

Appropriate background music played as the group comes together, or while setting up the safe space, will generate group harmony at many levels.

And finally, they will go round the circle, each in turn, to pick up their neighbour's colour. Suggest that, when it comes to their turn, they should try to project their colour to their neighbour and that their neighbour should keep an open mind to receive the colour. When the neighbour knows the colour, it is spoken aloud. The person projecting the colour answers 'Yes' or 'No'. The neighbour can try again, or can open it to the group. The leader can suggest that anyone who does not pick up the correct colour might like to put their hand out to the person projecting the colour to see how they feel. (Kinaesthetic people may well pick up the colour red as 'hot', blue as 'wet' or 'cool' and so on.)

Remind the group that some people are better at transmitting and others at receiving but that, with practice, both are possible. Encourage anyone who holds back to express what they feel – either what they are picking up or their own inner emotions. This helps them to trust the group and builds group cohesion.

EXERCISE
The rainbow group

- Sit with your eyes closed, feet on the floor and your hands resting loosely on

Remind the group that some people are better at transmitting and others at receiving.

your thighs. Breathe gently and easily. Breathe in for the count of five: one, two, three, four, five. Hold the breath for a slow count of three: one, two three. And breathe out for the count of six: one, two, three, four, five, six. And again – In: one, two, three, four, five. Hold: one, two, three. And out: one, two, three, four, five, six. And again – In: one, two, three, four, five. Hold: one, two, three. And out: one, two, three, four, five, six. Let that rhythm continue easily.

- Think of a colour. See that colour as a light above your head. The colour will come down from the light, filling your whole body and suffusing your biomagnetic field. Take the colour into the centre of your being. (Wait.)

- Look around the circle – with your eyes open or closed. There will be a rainbow all around you, each colour

connected to a member of the group. What colours do you see? (Wait.)

- Now bring your attention back to yourself and attune to your own colour once more.

- Now go around the circle. The leader asks the person on their right-hand side, 'What colour am I?'

• The person on the right of the leader names the colour. If it is not correct, another opportunity is given or it is thrown open to the group. When that colour has been established, move on, each person asking the person to their right, 'What colour am I?'

• When everyone in the group has completed their turn, the leader says: 'Now bring your attention back to yourself. Let your colour return to the light above your head. As it switches off, close your third-eye shield, and bring your attention back to your body and your awareness back into the room.'

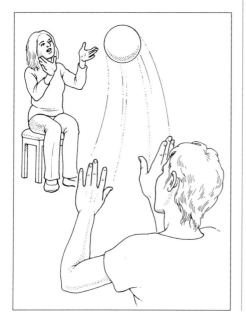

EXERCISE
Throwing the ball

Throwing the ball also uses colour. When the exercise begins, the ball goes around the circle, but as it progresses, it is tossed across the circle at random. The person throwing the ball calls the name of the person to whom it is going and visualizes the ball – the colour changes at random at it moves around the group.

The person receiving it calls out the colour they saw. The person who threw it says 'Yes' if correct, or if incorrect says 'No' and names the colour they were thinking of. Giving the colour enables people to see if their intuition is correct.

Strong transmitters

It may be that one, or more, members of the group are particularly strong transmitters. This can interfere with group exercises. If a group consistently seems to be getting the colours wrong, the leader should ask if anyone in the group is getting them all, or most, right. Ask that person to throw the ball and check how many people in the group picked up the colour. If most do, this is a person with a strong sending ability. That being the case, ask that person if they would mind stepping outside the room for a few moments and to refrain from thinking about the exercise. If the group gets more correct hits, the person who is out of the room, by apparently picking up a colour, is in fact sending it more strongly than the person who is throwing the ball. It would be helpful for the group if, during an exercise, that person deliberately refrained from naming or seeing a colour in their mind unless they were the sender.

However, if you do have a strong sender in your midst, you have an enormous asset. You can expand your telepathy games by asking that person to send from another room or a distant place while the group is together. You could also utilize the ability while the group is separate. Arrange a specific time when the group can all tune into the sender and have the sender transmit 20 colours, which individual members of the group pick up, everyone keeping a list. Next time the group meets, compare lists.

CHAPTER twelve

Intuitive dreaming

'One certainly ought
not to underestimate
the gigantic importance
of dreams.'

H.P. Lovecraft, *Beyond the Walls of Sleep*

the dream state

According to myth, dreams are the time when the soul leaves the body to wander in other realms. The Tibetans, who have been studying such matters for millennia, say that the realms the soul enters are those that it also encounters after death.

ALTERED STATES

A dream is an altered state of consciousness, as is a 'bliss' experience or hypnosis.
Characteristics of altered states are:

- Distorted sense of time
- Perceptual distortions
- Alterations in cognitive thinking
- Change in emotional expression
- Different meaning or significance
- Disassociation from, or unconsciousness of, the body

For the Tibetans, mastery of dream states means that, after death, the soul knows how to traverse these realms and is therefore freed from the pull of reincarnation.

As a dream is an altered state of consciousness, a dream may take only a moment or two of so-called real time, and yet last for hours, days, even weeks in dream time. It can move forward and backward in time, or operate outside it altogether. If you understand the stages and processes of sleeping and dreaming, you can use your dreams as a potent vehicle for your intuition.

The physiology of dreams

As the 20th century progressed, a great deal was learned about the physiology of dreams and dream sleep. By measuring the brain's electrical activity during sleep, a cycle of four stages were identified through the night. Three of them are non-REM sleep and one is the REM state.

The REM cycle dream

REM means rapid eye movement. It occupies 20–25 per cent of sleep, although the need for REM sleep decreases with age. Hypnagogic images and dreams occur in this lighter level of sleep, characterized by specific physiological signs and brainwave activity. REM sleep starts soon after you fall asleep. At this stage, it is fleeting and you quickly move through into the deeper stages. REM sleep occurs at approximately 90-minute intervals during the night but the period of REM sleep lengthens as the night progresses and is longest between 5 and 8 in the morning, when the body's physiological processes of food digestion and absorption should be complete. This is the most likely time for precognitive and lucid dreaming to occur as 'processing' or 'recycling' dreams takes place early on in the dream cycle.

A dream may take only a moment or two of so-called real time.

Sleep stage 1

Stage 1 (sleep onset and active sleep phase) is characterized by low amplitude, fast EEG pattern, frequency 8–12 cycles per second, alpha, beta or delta waves may be present. Hypnagogic images: fast, fleeting, flowing. Myclonic movements: jerking, feeling of falling. Moves into REM sleep and dreaming.

Sleep stages 2 & 3

Higher amplitude, lower frequency delta and theta waves. May contain random thoughts and slight movement.

Sleep stage 4

Inert sleep, slow brainwaves, 4–8 Hz, characterized by 'spindles' in the brain's electrical pattern. Approximately 50 per cent theta waves.

These stages cycle throughout the night, with REM sleep increasing in length. Research has shown that, during a dream, brain cells fire as they would during a conscious experience, with two crucial differences. Movement during sleep is inhibited and external sensory input to

REM SLEEP

Rem sleep is characterized by:
- Rapid Eye Movements
- Shallow, rapid breathing
- Slow pulse
- Alteration in muscle tone
- Changes in facial muscles
- Decreased spinal reflexes
- Nasal dilation
- Emotional arousal
- Genital arousal in men and women

the cortex of the brain is restricted – although feelings of cold, heat and so on can be transferred into a dream. Memory and emotion continue. The subtle subliminal perceptions of ESP – and the ability to move around in time – are incorporated into a dream as imagery or memory but rarely into physical movement.

Dream chemicals

The German biochemist Otto Loewi, a Nobel Prize winner, experimented with the vagus nerve. Stimulated electrically, the nerve slowed the heart and Loewi theorized that a chemical was responsible. Unsure how to prove this, a dream showed him the way. Stimulating the vagus nerve of a frog, he took its blood and injected it into another frog, whose heart slowed. Isolated and analyzed, the chemical, the neurotransmitter acetylocholine, induced dream sleep and improved cognitive functioning. It occurs naturally in lecithin but needs vitamins B1 and 5 for assimilation.

Vitamin B6 (found in meat, salmon, herring, brewer's yeast, cabbage, soya, broad beans, pears, bananas, green vegetables, wheat germ, molasses, wholegrains and egg) and nutmeg have also been shown to induce dreams and promote recall.

Dream partnership

Researchers observing sleepers wake them whenever rapid eye movements are discerned. Dreams accessed during the early part of the night are unlikely to be intuitive or lucid. A partner who wakes early, waits until your rapid eye movements cease and wakes you gently, asking 'What were you dreaming?', is the best aid you can have to intuitive, and especially lucid, dreaming.

the psychology of dreams

Throughout the last century, psychoanalysts were fascinated by dreams, believing that these were a pathway into their patient's unconscious mind. Analyzing dreams threw light on inner processes and unfulfilled wishes.

According to Freud, deep-seated desires and primal images from a dark layer of the psyche slid into dreams, sanitized and disguised. Many of these were black impulses that could not be voiced in the light. There was little room for intuition. For Jung, dreams were full of symbolism and imagery, much of which came from a collective rather than a personal level but which nevertheless could be intuition speaking.

An opposite view said that dreams merely processed what had happened during the day – a kind of mental re-cycling bin. Those who thought in this way saw little of value in exploring the meaning of dreams further.

'Premature closure'

Dreamwork practitioners now believe that dreams have, among other things, the function of drawing attention to where our thinking has prematurely solidified. As Jeremy Taylor put it: 'It's comfortable to think we know it all and that we have everything sussed. But dreams challenge our assumptions, point out where we've sold ourselves short or made a mistake.'

When this occurs, dreams purvey messages from the intuitive mind. A woman dreamt, for example, that she was on a snowmobile, travelling over ice alongside her ex-partner. He zoomed on ahead and disappeared down a crevasse. For a while she remained detached, watching to see if he would reappear. She became very agitated and went to see if she could help. Eventually he appeared from a totally different direction, completely frozen. She immediately found herself thinking: 'If only I'd gone down sooner, I might have saved him. I didn't do enough.'

When she woke she realized that she had slipped back into an old pattern. Her relationship had broken up when she became seriously ill with a heart condition and realized that her partner's frozen emotional attitude toward her was breaking her heart. It had taken her months of work to detach herself. Feeling she had 'done it', she had relaxed.

The dream graphically showed her that she was being pulled in again. Her ex-partner was working on her new house and was unloading all his emotional angst onto her once more. She was trying to help him get in touch with his feelings – frozen feelings he had no intention of facing. She rapidly detached herself.

the metaphysics of dreams

When Edmond Rostand asked: 'What is life,
without a dream?', he may not have had intuition in mind, but he
was asking a profound question.

Metaphysicians and mystics often believe that life is a dream and that dreams can give you a glimpse of a greater reality. C.G. Jung had a dream that reflected this. In his dream he was a butterfly dreaming that he was a man on earth who was dreaming that he was a butterfly. Jung asked which was the true reality.

Intuitive dreams offer guidance and show what is to come. Inducing dreams was a standard healing practice in ancient Egypt and Greece and they have been used down through the ages to gain insight. Many famous inventors and scientists solved their difficulties intuitively through their dreams.

Dreaming solutions

When the chemist Kekule could not understand how the formula he had found for benzine could possibly be correct, he daydreamed the answer. Seeing a snake swallowing its tail showed him that it was a ring. It was not the only time his answer arrived in a dream. Asleep on a bus, he dreamed of pairs of atoms attracting others 'in a frenzied dance'. He had found the basis of atomic structure. Dmitri Mendeleyev spent many months

working out the Periodic Table of Elements, the basis for modern chemistry. But its ultimate form was revealed to him in a dream. Elias Howe, inventor of the sewing machine, was having problems with designing the needle. He dreamed he was being chased by cannibals carrying spears with holes in the end. He repositioned the hole to the tip of the needle, and the sewing machine was born.

Creative dreams

Dreams can be an important part of the creative process. Milton, the 17th-century

TESTING TRUTH

Before you go to sleep, sit with a straight spine. Picture with your third eye an old-fashioned pair of scales. On the left-hand pan, place the situation you wish to know the truth about. On the right-hand pan, place the feather of Maat. The pans may quickly move into balance, which indicates that the situation is in accord with cosmic harmony. They may continue to swing, which indicates that the situation is still being weighed up. If the pan with the situation on immediately sinks to the bottom, it is not in accord with truth. (If you are kinaesthetic use your hands as the scales with an actual feather and something to represent the situation.) Petition Maat that, by tomorrow, the truth of the situation will be revealed. Tell yourself that if the answer comes in a dream you will remember it but that you are open to the truth revealing itself in an appropriate way.

poet, put reason aside and 'wrote in his sleep'. When he awoke 'his muse' would have given him 30 lines or so, which he used his reason to refine. Milton recorded that his inspiration was: '… not to be obtained by the invocation of Dame Memory and her Siren daughters, but by devout prayer to that eternal Spirit who can enrich with all utterance and knowledge, and sends out his seraphim, with the hallowed fire of his altar, to touch and purify the lips of whom he pleases.' Devout prayer, as with REM sleep, produces an altered state of consciousness in which intuition can be accessed.

The life-saving dream

A dream may be precognitive. This does not necessarily mean that what you see will come to pass – it can be symbolic. Notwithstanding, it may be a timely warning that allows you to change the future.

Many years ago, I had a vivid dream. I was working for a sceptical scientist but, as he featured in it, I felt compelled to tell him. In my dream he and his wife were driving along a quiet country road when suddenly a car hurtled toward them on the wrong side of the road, into a head-on collision. No one could get out alive from a crash like that. I woke up extremely upset and weeping.

After the weekend, a very shaken man stood at my desk. 'Yesterday my wife was driving. I looked at the road and thought: "This is the road Judy described." At that moment a car came hurtling down the road toward us, on the wrong side. I grabbed the wheel and steered us onto the grass verge, shouting at my wife to brake. Thanks to you, we managed to avoid a head-on collision.' Knowing what was coming allowed him to avoid what would otherwise have been inevitable.

remembering your dreams

Everyone dreams. But not everyone remembers. However,
you can programme yourself to remember. Each night, before you go to sleep,
repeat three times: 'I remember my dream when I awake.'

AIDS TO REMEMBERING

- Vitamin B6
- Nutmeg
- Clary sage essential oil in a good quality carrier oil, lightly rubbed on the third eye, temples and base of neck
- Green jade or red jasper taped on your forehead or placed under your pillow
- Abstain from alcohol or drugs

Tell yourself that, whenever you have had a significant dream, you will naturally awake so that you can record it. Train yourself to wake up 15 minutes before the alarm clock goes off so that you will have time to recollect and record your dreams in tranquillity. If you can hear a chiming clock, awake when the clock strikes six or seven, and remember.

The throat chakra connection

Research has confirmed what Tibetan Dream Yoga has known for hundreds of years. Stimulating the rear throat chakra and its connection with the brain-stem activates the dream state.

Focus your attention on the back of your throat. Picture a bright white light activating this point and passing through to the stem of your brain. As you do this, drink a glass of water or hot chocolate with added nutmeg.

When you awake
- Do not move
- Pay attention to your thoughts and dream memories that go through your head
- Record your dream with the minimum of movement possible

Recording tools
- Voice-activated tape recorder
- Easy-flowing pen
- Intuition Journal
- Torch or small light

Recording your dreams
Although some dreams involve the brain, those that take place away from the body or are intuitive have to pass through the brain to be remembered. As soon as you awake, record your dream in your

Intuition Journal, (keep this especially close to your bedside) or tape them. If you use a voice-activated machine, you can keep your eyes closed and make the minimum of movement (research shows that movement destroys dream memory). Keep the light level low. Record everything, without embroidering, judging or censoring – even fragments or odd words. The smallest details could turn out to be significant.

Some people like to record the main events of their day briefly before going to sleep so that they can immediately recognize any connection with the dreams they have that night.

Exercise
Ritual dreaming

Using ritual can stimulate dreams. In ancient times, temples were dedicated to dreaming. The more involved your body is in the ritual, the better chance it has of succeeding. Make all your movements slow and deliberate. Rituals work better at certain times than others, so choose your time. Menstruating women should experiment to see which part of their

The more involved your body is in the ritual, the better chance it has of succeeding.

cycle is most fertile for dreaming – it is often the middle. The dark of the moon was a traditional time for going within and dreaming, but placing moonstone or selenite under your pillow at the full moon can stimulate a powerful dream. Make your dream ritual a special occasion. Note the dates on your calendar in advance so that your intuition can get to work out of time. You will need:

- Rose or clary sage oil
- Candles
- Crystals
- Herb pillow containing lavender or mugwort (*artemisia vulgaris*) Warning: avoid mugwort if pregnant.
- Hot chocolate with added nutmeg

Take a long leisurely bath to which you have added rose or clary sage oil. Burn candles and gaze into an appropriate

INCUBATING A DREAM

If you need guidance on a particular subject, incubate a dream. Choose a night when you can take time in the morning to process the dream. Abstain from alcohol or drugs and, if you wish, perform the dream ritual. Contemplate the issue on which you need dream guidance. Look at the solutions you have already tried, the action you have taken. Ask yourself whether you are ready to resolve it. If there are emotional issues, are you prepared to let go? Tell yourself that when you awake, you will remember the answering dream. Then put it aside and sleep. As soon as you wake up, write down your dream in your dream journal.

crystal. Programme it so that when you place it under your pillow, it will help you to dream true and wisely. Use the throat chakra activation, drinking your spiced hot chocolate. Dress in clean night attire. Place the herb pillow on top of your usual pillows so that you are sleeping higher than normal on your right side. Place your crystal under the herb pillow. As you go to sleep, picture yourself entering the dream temple.

Expanding a dream

Dream dialogue is a powerful way to expand an intuitive dream, especially if the dream seems to be incomplete or foreshortened by premature awakening.

EXERCISE
Dream dialogue

Close your eyes and go back into your dream at the point where it left off. Look at the dream from the standpoint of one of the characters – yourself if you featured in the dream. Ask questions: 'What is the meaning of this?', 'What insight does it give me?', 'What am I hiding from myself?', 'Where will this take me?' Question other characters: 'Why are you doing that?', 'What does it signify?', 'Do you have any guidance for me?' Then step into the shoes of another character (it does not have to be a person). Ask the same questions. Let the dream run on and see how it ends.

Interpreting your intuitive dreams

The meaning of some intuitive dreams will be immediately apparent, while others are shrouded in mystery. Quietly contemplate your dream and ask your intuitive mind to clarify it. Say: 'If I were to know what this means, it would be …' Allow answers and images to arise spontaneously. If the answer does not come within five minutes or so, put it aside. Often the answer makes itself known as soon as you stop focusing on it.

A guide to traditional dream meanings is shown overleaf, but the most useful interpretation is the one that arises spontaneously from your own intuitive mind (ulexite crystal can aid understanding). Dreams may contain puns, colloquialisms, body language and symbolism that are personal to you, and many of the characters symbolize parts of yourself, for instance, dreaming that you have a pain in the neck may indicate that someone is a pain to be around. Places can indicate your state of mind and weather can represent your emotions. So, when you record your dream, add anything else it brings to mind – connections, word plays, similarities and so on. Look for themes that link to previous dreams and to situations you are currently involved in. Notice images from your recent past and people you know or characters who remind you of people you have known, and what the dream behaviour tells you.

The meaning of some intuitive dreams will be immediately apparent, while others are shrouded in mystery.

prophetic dream meanings

SYMBOL	PROPHETIC MEANING
Abyss/avalanche	Danger/something rising into consciousness
Abandoned	Excluded/leaving things behind
Abduction	No control
Accident to head	Recklessness/danger to oneself or father
Accident to right foot	Danger to siblings
Accident to left foot	Danger to servants/employees
Accident to right hand	Danger to mother
Accident to left hand	Danger to children
Accused by man	Good news/inner saboteur
Accused by woman	Bad news/inner saboteur
Actor	Role play/deceit, falseness
Aeroplane	Ambition, success
Alcohol	Shutting off feelings
Alien	Unacknowledged part of self
Altar	Consolation, joy
Ambulance	Wound, illness
Ambush	Betrayal
Amputation	Body pun – 'haven't a leg to stand on'
Anchor	Attachment/grounding
Angel	Protection, happiness
Anger	Reconciliation
Applause	Reproach/need self-acknowledgement
Army	Obstacles
Arrow/archery	Direction
Baby	Luck in the home/new birth
Bag/barrel, full	Abundance
Bag/barrel, empty	Poverty/poverty consciousness
Ball	Opportunity
Ball, rolling	Success delayed

Barking	Beware	Bread, brown/stale	Worry
Basement	Anguish/torment/hidden thoughts	Bridge	Happy solution
		Burial	Early marriage
Bathing	Purification/feeling unclean	Burial (one's own)	Serious illness/new beginning
Battle	Illness		
Beard, cut	Illness	Butterfly	Inconstancy/rebirth
Beard, fair	Good counsel	Cage, empty	Marriage break-up/release
Beard, black	Betrayal	Cage, full	Fear/feeling trapped
Bed, made	Rest	Cake	Family festivities
Bed, unmade	Mistakes	Cat	Deceit
Bed, empty	Disappointment	Castle	Happy event
Bees, alive	Good fortune/helpful friends	Cemetery	News of death
Bees, dead	Loss of money/ untrustworthy friends	Chair	Position/attitude
		Chased	Being haunted by something, longing to escape
Bell/birds	Good news		
Bicycle	Early success	Chocolate	Satisfaction
Birdcage	Slander	Chilblains	Indiscretion
Blindness	Deceit/betrayal	Clock	Important business
Blood	Vitality/energy drain	Clothes	Persona/attitudes
Bouquet	Disappointment	Cradle	Hope realized
Bottle	Bottled up/clarity	Crime, witness	Exaggerated fear
Bottle, broken	Quarrel	Crab	Separation
Boat	Fortunate journey	Death (one's own)	Good health, transformation, fresh start
Bread, white/fresh	Good luck coming		

Dice	Loss	Hand	Flattery
Dog	Faithful love	Horse, white	Wealth
Drunkenness	Certain success	Horse, black	Pleasure following sorrow
Eagle	Prosperity	Hospital	Distress/healing
Earthquake	Change or fear of change	House	Situations/parts of yourself
Eggs	Abundance	Illness	Dis-ease
Eyes, beautiful	Love	Jewels	Money/inner riches
Eyes, lost	Death of a relative	Jewels, imitation	Vanity
Feather	Frivolity	Key	Missed appointment/insight
Fireplace with fire	Family pleasures	Kiss	Deceit/new relationship
Fireplace, smoking	Quarrel	Kitten	New projects
Fire, out	Sorrow	Lawyer	Lawsuit, poverty
Flag/flame	Success/passion	Ladder	Up, success/down, failure
Flying/falling	Anxiety/OOBE	Labyrinth	Mystery revealed
Fork	Choices/change of direction	Lantern	Be prudent/inner light
Frog	Indiscretion		needed
Garden	Pleasant surprise	Letter	Neglect of friendship/news
Gambling	Good if losing, bad if	Lion	Powerful adversary/protector
	winning	Lighthouse	Protection
Going up	Improvement or success	Lock, broken	Theft
Going down	Reversal of fortune	Luggage	Trip/inner baggage
Gold	Inner riches	Maps	Long journey
Hair	Trickery	Matches, burning	Success
Hat	Disillusionment	Mask	Lies

Playing cards	Loss of money		weighing up matters
Moon, full	Delay	School	Life's lessons
Moon, misty	Illness	Sea	Calm, happiness/rough, anger/Intuition
Mouse	Loss of money lent		
Object, shiny	Good omens	Shaving	Loss of money
Object, dirty	Obstacles	Snake	A grudge against you
Owl	Delay beginning	Tent	Unforeseen adventure
Pin	Wounded self-esteem	Thunderstorm	Danger threatens
Police/authority figure	Control	Throne	Change of position
Postman	Letter on way	Thief	False friend
Puppet	Manipulation	Tomb	Long life
Purse	Full, loss of profit/empty, money coming	Umbrella	Lasting friendship
		Umbrella, found	Valuable connection
Rainbow	End of troubles	Undressing	Lack of foresight
Removal	Change of employment	Upsetting something	Upset or overturn
Ring	Engagement/marriage	Veil, torn	Secrets revealed
Ring, broken	Divorce	Vomit	Great worry/something coming up
Road	Broad, happy life/narrow, deceit		
		Waterfall	Purification/release
Ruins	Reverses of fortune	Wave	Acknowledgement/ connection
Scissors	Release		
	Quarrel, death of friend/cutting free	Wealth	Disillusion
		Weather	Emotional state
Scales	Legal business/	Weeping	Good news

dreaming with awareness

Lucid dreams are an ideal vehicle for your intuitive awareness. In a lucid dream, you know you are dreaming and can cooperate or intervene in events. These powerful dreams can transform your life.

A lucid dream is a dream in which you are aware that you are dreaming and, as you become adept, can influence the course of the dream. Many lucid dreams start, or end, as flying dreams and may be linked with out-of-body experiences (see page 53). Dreaming with awareness is extremely powerful and can have great healing properties. It expands personal reality and transcends limitations. You become aware of the nature of your true self. Skilful lucid dreaming means that waking consciousness can be maintained during dreams, and dream awareness can be carried into waking consciousness.

Facilitating a lucid dream

Researchers into lucid dreaming use a red strobe light to remind a dreamer that he or she is dreaming. But there are ancient techniques for inducing lucid dreaming.

Hand signals

While intuitive and lucid dreams usually take place away from the physical body, in the dream you will nonetheless usually have a dream-body. The classic way of inducing a lucid dream, taught across all traditions for thousands of years, uses a body signal. Before you go to sleep, tell yourself that when you see your hand (or your feet) in a dream, you will know that you are dreaming and will continue the dream in a lucid way.

Programme a lucid dream

As you fall asleep tell yourself: 'I am aware I am dreaming, I am conscious of my dream. I know I am dreaming. I step into my dream.'

Tibetan Dream Yoga

Tibetan Dream Yoga is an ancient way of facilitating and gaining control of a lucid dream. Practitioners are not allowed to lie down. They are put in boxes too small to

Many lucid dreams start, or end, as flying dreams and may be linked with out-of-body experiences.

stretch out in. Prop yourself on pillows, on your right side, and place a brick wrapped in a towel at your feet so you cannot stretch out to simulate this method.

Crystal lucidity

Use danburite or moonstone, especially at full moon. An elixir made from the stone is particularly effective if sipped before you go to bed.

Awaken yourself

Researchers found that waking up two hours earlier than you would normally rise, getting up and being active for an hour or two, and then going back to bed, instigates lucid dreaming. Once you become adept, shorten the period you are awake until lucid dreaming arises naturally during sleep.

When you awaken from an early-morning dream, go over the dream, telling yourself that next time you dream, you will be aware. Let yourself fall back to sleep.

Visualize as you fall sleep – you can find yourself stepping effortlessly from visualization into a lucid dream. Go into your favourite place (see page 128) and proceed from there.

Put yourself into alpha

Visualize your name printed in dots, and then the words 'LUCID DREAM', to induce alpha brainwaves.

Controlling a lucid dream

Once you become aware that you are dreaming, remind yourself that you are. At regular intervals say: 'This is a dream.' You can go along with the dream while you get used to the situation. As with out-of-body experiences, you can direct yourself to different places. Some people find that closing their dream-body eyes and opening them again transports them to where they want to go (it may take you back to your bed; if so, remind yourself it is not time to wake up and move away again). It is easier at first to make small, gradual changes and to use the people you meet in your dreams to assist you.

The people you meet may surprise you. It can be helpful to remind yourself that you are dreaming and that this is your experience. These people have no independent life within your dream, you are dreaming them. However, you can use their wisdom and expertise to solve problems, and find creative possibilities, obtain healing and guidance. A powerful technique, once you are an adept, is to call into your dream anyone with whom you have a problem. Working it out in your dreams will transpose into your outer life. You can also use a lucid dream as a rehearsal for an event still to come.

MEETING THE DREAM HEALER

If you have a problem with your health, you can invite into your dream a dream healer to give you exactly the treatment you need for maximum well-being. Some of the treatments can be unusual, to say the least, but remind yourself that you are dreaming. The benefit when you wake is worth whatever it takes in the dream. Use the technique for meeting your mentor (see page 155) or for entering a hospital building or healing temple to meet your healer. (This technique can be adapted for any situation where you require assistance or knowledge from the dream mentor or teacher.)

CHAPTER thirteen

Divination tools

'Casting a spread and conducting a reading can bring an extraordinary level of clarity, awareness, and illumination.'

David Lawson, *The Eye of Horus*

aiding intuition

Divination tools act as a focus for your intuition. They help you to empty your mind of everything but the situation you are asking about. The question is, which one will aid you?

There are literally hundreds of tarot packs, oracles and divination aids. While initially you will probably follow your chosen system rigidly, and may need to consult books of meaning, with practice the symbols will come to have a personal meaning for you. This is when your intuition will really take off.

Identifying which tools work best for you

A divination tool that is in harmony with the way your intuition functions will clearly be the most effective. If you are kinaesthetic, handling and laying out sticks, cards or runes is tactile and sets up optimum conditions for your intuition. If you are visual, it will be symbols and patterns that speak to you, and you may enjoy tarot cards and the like. If your intuition is auditory, you may well hear an inner voice speak to you as you lay out cards or cast the *I Ching*. If you have a logical, analytical mind, you will find that a divination tool such as numerology or astrology satisfies your need for order.

The easiest way to choose your divination tool is to go to a store that offers a wide range of possibilities. Take a look at cards, runes and the *I Ching* (the *Book of Changes*). Read a numerology or astrology book. See what resonates with you. Browse through an illustrated divination book and note which images catch your eye (see the bibliography). Get together a group of your friends to buy a few tools and experiment with them.

Dedicating and programming tools

No matter which tools you select to enhance your intuition, they will be easier to use and will speak more truly if you take the time to dedicate and programme them. Keep them wrapped in a silk scarf or wooden box when not in use. Do not let other people handle your tools, except to shuffle them for a reading.

To cleanse a divination tool

Using a smudge stick, pass the divination tool through the smoke. If you do not have a smudge stick, you can use the light from a candle.

To dedicate a divination tool

Hold the divination tool in your hands. Say out loud: 'I dedicate this tool to the highest good of all who consult it and declare that it will speak only truth and light forever more.'

With practice the symbols will come to have a personal meaning for you.

tarot and cartomancy

The origins of the tarot are unknown, but the first recognized pack of tarot cards comes from Italy and dates from the fifteenth century and was used in a somewhat complicated card game similar to bridge.

The images on tarot cards incorporate universal symbols, or archetypes, that speak across all cultures and times. The tarot is a subtle, multi-layered method of divination. At their most superficial, they are used for fortune-telling but, when properly understood, they give powerful insights into your life.

The cards are divided into the major and minor arcana. There are 22 major cards, each attuned to a different archetypal experience. These can stand alone for readings, and may be used as a system of spiritual initiation. Images such as The Lovers are fairly obvious as to their interpretation – relationships – but cards such as Death are often misunderstood. This is the card of endings and major changes or, when reversed, stagnation. It rarely portends an actual death. The minor cards are divided into four suits, each associated with a different area of life, and give added depth to a reading.

Symbolic meanings

Tarot cards are excellent for people who resonate with imagery and symbolism, but they also appeal to those who like 'touchy, feely' sensations. The act of shuffling and laying out the cards is kinaesthetic. There are a number of layouts that can be used for general or more specialized information and the sheer number of different packs available means that almost everyone will find a tarot pack that speaks to them.

Cartomancy

You do not have to purchase a special tarot pack, however. Ordinary playing cards can be used for divination. Modern playing cards arose out of the tarot and there is a resonance between the suits and the minor arcana (the major having been dropped). Diamonds relate to money and the material world, while hearts deal with emotion, romance and relationships. Clubs indicate prestige, influence and enterprise, while spades, traditionally associated with conflict and misfortune, can give a timely warning.

As with the tarot, playing cards represent particular traits, personalities and areas of life. They can be used to investigate the future, or to explore the influences operating in your life – some of which may not yet have come to your attention. They may also show someone who is passing into or out of your life.

numerology

*The Greek mathematician Pythagoras taught that number was the
essence of all things. Each number had a specific and unique resonance and
that mathematics could help us understand the universe.*

Your birth date produces your most basic and fundamental number, the life number. A dominating influence throughout your life, it indicates your life purpose and denotes lessons you have to learn, which may be modified by unfolding cycles but which will always form part of your inner being.

To find your life number, add together the individual digits of your birth date, including the birth year in full, until reduced to a single digit. (Note, however, that 11 and 22 are master numbers that have their own interpretation.)

What number are you?

1   Self and reasoning mind. Positive:
    Energetic, confident, creative,
    outgoing. Natural leader, strong will.
    Likes control. May dominate.
    Negative: Addiction, frustration,
    insecurity, wilfulness, egotism,
    intolerance.

2   Spirit of cooperation and harmony.
    Positive: Supportive, caring, sensitive,
    efficient. Needs security and stability.
    Passive and receptive, natural assistant.
    Negative: Over-critical, indecisive,
    over-adapting, overly servile, helps
    then suddenly withdraws.

3 Urge for emotional expression.
Positive: Sensitive, active, sociable,
articulate. Successful. Inspired.
Idealistic, eternal optimist. Negative:
Fear of rejection, compulsive
attention-seeker, conceit, deceit,
depression, over-sensitivity.

4 Form and matter. Positive: Logical,
secure, reliable, dependable. Calmly
efficient, makes patient progress.
Negative: Reserved, rigid. Unstable,
impatient, impractical, fixed in ways.

5 Balance between freedom and
discipline. Positive: Freedom-loving,
energetic, spontaneous, restless.
Multifaceted. Lively. Versatile
communicator. Negative: Scattered,
irresponsible, over-cautious, unreliable.

6 Love. Positive: Comforting, diplomatic,
accepting. Giving, caring. Seeks
balance and harmony. Excellent in
business, money. Negative:

Perfectionism, self-indulgence,
selfishness, possessiveness, jealousy.

7 Need to develop trust. Positive:
Meditative, introverted, aloof.
Journeying inward, dreams of better
world. Discriminating, analytical,
observative. Negative: Suspicion,
escapism, bitterness, betrayal.

8 Need to integrate material success
and spiritual attainment. Positive:
Generous, determined, trustworthy.
Good organizer, likes control.
Negative: Demanding, sabotages self,
slave-driver, obsessive about money.

9 Completion. Positive: Dynamic,
charismatic, independent. Evolved soul;
needs self-understanding. Negative:
Selfish, dissipates talents, bigotry.

11 On a mission. Powerful leader,
formidable enemy. Persuasive.

22 Special person. Strong, masterful.
Enormous potential if handled well.

astrology

Although often derided, astrology gained some academic credence when the Frenchman Michel Gauquelin tried to match people's professions to their star sign - and proved that there was a correlation.

strology works with unfolding cycles. The zodiac tells the story of incarnation into matter, the birth of the ego, and the progression back to the whole. Taking a symbolic picture of the heavens at the moment you were born, astrology unfolds it throughout your life.

Your birth chart is a map of your life, your potential and your personality. It provides a deeply insightful picture of your strengths and weaknesses, your abilities and your foibles. It pinpoints moments of opportunity and change. An intuitive astrologer will know exactly how

to work with those cycles and the influences of the planets. A good astrologer intuits exactly how far you have gone toward fulfilling your chart – and how you can overcome any blockages.

As everyone born on the same day in the same place at the same time has the same birth chart, intuition is needed to tune into the individual soul behind the chart. By attuning to the energies of the planets and zodiac signs, moving beyond text-book definitions of what they mean, astrologers resonate with the effect of the universe on the individual at any given moment. They can take this forward or backward in time. Understanding the past brings meaning to the present, and looking at what is to come also illuminates the present.

Astrology appeals to both the intuitive mind and logical minds. Once you get over the apparent illogicality of the heavens influencing life on earth, the sheer weight of evidence of over 4,000 years of observation of the correspondences between the heavens and human behaviour is overwhelming. The myths and archetypes embodied in astrology cover the whole of human history and experience. A scientific mind enjoys the precision of calculation and tables. An intuitive mind relishes moving beyond them. For people who are kinaesthetic, astrology can be brought alive through drama and movement.

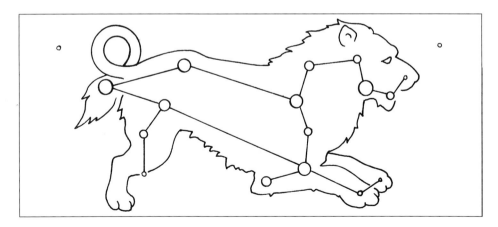

THE I CHING HEXAGRAMS

1 Reduction

9 Little progress

17 Pursuit

25 The unexpected

33 Retreat

41 Reduction

49 Revolution

57 Willing submission

2 Willing submission

10 Caution

18 Work on what is spoilt

26 Taking control

34 Strength

42 Increase

50 Cauldren

58 Joy

3 Gestation

11 Peace

19 Approach slowly

27 Watchful waiting

35 Progress

43 Breakthrough

51 Thunderclaps

59 Dispersing

4 Growth

12 Obstruction

20 Watchfulness

28 Excess

36 Darkening light

44 Meeting

52 Stillness

60 Restriction

5 Calculated inaction

13 Lovers

21 Biting through

29 The Abyss

37 Family

45 Joining together

53 Progress

61 Inner truth

6 Conflict

14 Abundance

22 Grace

30 Shining brightly

38 Opposition

46 Moving up

54 Marrying maiden

62 Stay small

7 Battle

15 Modesty

23 Splitting apart

31 Attraction

39 Obstruction

47 Adversity

55 Fullness

63 Final completion

8 Unity

16 Repose

24 Turning point

32 Enduring

40 Disentangling

48 The well

56 The traveller

64 Not yet complete

i ching

The I Ching *is an extremely ancient oracle said to describe heaven, earth and all that happens within them. It is based on the idea that everything is in flux and motion.*

The traditional method of consulting the *I Ching* uses 49 yarrow stalks, revealing 64 possible hexagrams. Nowadays, many people use coins to produce those same hexagrams. It is possible that psychokinesis is involved in the fall of the stalks or coins.

The *I Ching* is excellent at pinpointing moments of change and showing how to make the most of them. It makes visible what lies behind the façade of everyday life and can help with timing events. The pattern of the *I Ching* hexagrams stimulates insights and perceptions, moving you beyond the surface meaning. They appeal to people who are visual and those who prefer to touch, because the ritual of using the *I Ching* mellows and focuses consciousness through an orderly set of movements. To make a simple hexagram:

- Throw a coin onto a flat surface
- Heads represent an unbroken, yang line _____
- Tails represent a broken, yin line __ __
- Write down your line as the base line above which you will build up five more lines
- Repeat five more times, placing each line above the other.

runes & chiromancy

Both runes and chiromancy are tools that enable you to get in touch with your intuition. Both are based on ancient wisdom and enable you to ask meaningful questions about your life, or about another's.

Chiromancy

Chiromancy, or palmistry, looks to the lines on the hands to read fate, fortune and character. It maps out your life span, your relationships and your health. A baby is born with lines on its palms, which set out its destiny. However, palms change and show how a person is developing. Nothing is fixed, and making the most of your potential can overcome the most difficult of palms. One hand tends to remain the same, showing what you are born with, while the other hand changes as you mature and go through your life experiences.

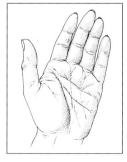

The lines on the palm 'speak' to a visual person, providing a map that can be read as easily as a book. If you are a kinaesthetic person, you may well find that chiromancy brings out your natural intuition. As you hold a person's hand, you will tune into their energies. The lines on the palm merely confirm what you intuit.

The word rune means 'secret writing', and the symbols are imbued with magical power. They were said to have appeared

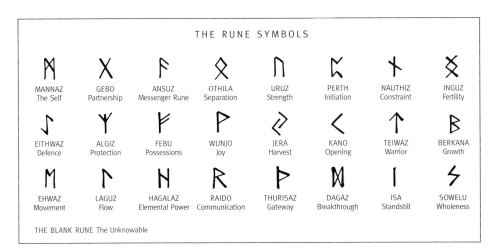

THE RUNE SYMBOLS

MANNAZ
The Self

GEBO
Partnership

ANSUZ
Messenger Rune

OTHILA
Separation

URUZ
Strength

PERTH
Initiation

NAUTHIZ
Constraint

INGUZ
Fertility

EITHWAZ
Defence

ALGIZ
Protection

FEBU
Possessions

WUNJO
Joy

JERA
Harvest

KANO
Opening

TEIWAZ
Warrior

BERKANA
Growth

EHWAZ
Movement

LAGUZ
Flow

HAGALAZ
Elemental Power

RAIDO
Communication

THURISAZ
Gateway

DAGAZ
Breakthrough

ISA
Standstill

SOWELU
Wholeness

THE BLANK RUNE The Unknowable

to the Norse god Odin while he was hung upside down in the World Tree.

Sitting quietly with the runes helps you to go deep inside yourself. Most have a double meaning, depending on whether they are upright or reversed. They can describe positive and negative influences operating in your life. Selecting three will show past, present and future influences and outcomes. Picking one at random will reveal your innermost fears and desires. They map the path of spiritual initiation, and can help you to make positive choices for the future. Runes are a particularly tactile experience. Most are made of natural materials – wood or stone. Placed in a bag, one or more will 'stick' to your fingers. These are the runes for you.

crystals for intuition

Crystals have been used to enhance intuition for thousands of years. Ancient graves contain crystal mirrors, jewellery and crystal balls. They are still useful divination tools today.

The high priests of Israel and Egypt wore breastplates adorned with crystals, shamans and sorcerers placed them on their magical instruments, and seers peered into their inner depths. Methods of divination like scrying with a crystal ball go back into antiquity. Gazing into a crystal ball frees your rational mind and focuses your intuition. Crystals can put you in touch with your inner guidance, or attune you to something greater.

Crystals to enhance Intuition

Your intuition can be developed by holding amethyst, amazonite, ametrine, apophyllite, antacamite, or aqua aura to your third eye for a few moments daily, or by meditating with the crystal in place. This is particularly useful when you begin scrying or when you are seeking guidance. You can also meditate by gazing into crystal. Wear crystal earrings to heighten your intuition. The following crystals also enhance inuition:

Azeztulite, azurite with malachite, celestite, herkimer diamond, kyanite, lavender smithsonite, lapis lazuli, moonstone, petalite, phantom quartz, star sapphire, selenite, smoky quartz, sodalite, and yellow calcite.

Crystals to close off mind chatter
Blue selenite or rhomboid calcite

Crystals to induce dreaming
Amethyst, selenite, blue howlite, bloodstone, celestite, charoite, rhodocrosite or moonstone.

Crystal scrying
Scrying means looking to the future. Many people use a crystal ball for this, but any transparent crystal or cluster can be used. Quartz, amethyst, beryl and obsidian have traditionally been used but apophyllite gives excellent results. A crystal with internal planes and flaws helps your inner eye to see images within it. Keep the crystal specially for the purpose, and do not allow other people to handle it unless you are reading for them as the crystal will pick up vibrations and impressions. When not in use, keep your crystal wrapped in a cloth.

If it is the first time you have used your crystal, it should be cleansed by holding it under running water or leaving it in salt overnight if friable. It should be dedicated by holding it in your hands and stating that it is dedicated to the highest good and that it will always speak true. (Remember to cleanse your crystal from time to time.)

Exercise
Reading the crystal
- Settle down where you will not be disturbed. Use candlelight to create a soft atmosphere. If you have a specific question, formulate this beforehand and keep it in your mind. Hold the crystal in your hands or put it on a table in front of you if it is heavy. Gaze at the crystal but do not try to see anything yet. Let your eyes go out of focus – they need to be gentle if your inner eye is to open. Breathe

quietly, setting up a natural rhythm.

- As your eyes loosen, allow them to explore the crystal. You may see mist forming in the crystal. When the mist clears, it will form images or you may see scenes as though a film is running in the crystal. You may see a static or moving symbol. Pictures may form in your mind rather than in the crystal. If you see a symbol, ask if it is positive or negative. Positive images tend to be bright, negative images dimmer and darker.

- If you are kinaesthetic, you may get feelings or body sensations: these will be the answer from the crystal.

IMAGE	POSITIVE INTERPRETATION	NEGATIVE INTERPRETATION
Bird	A message on its way	Escapism
Cat	Good prospects	Trouble brewing
Dog	Trustworthy friends	Deceitful friends
Eye	Good luck	Bad luck
Globe	Travel	Stagnation
House	Well-being	Financial problems
Moon	New growth	Disappointment
Snake	Learning	Betrayal
Star	Success	Warning
Tree	Settling down	Loss

casting the stones

A fast method of scrying when you do not have the time or the opportunity for a crystal reading is to use tumbled stones in a bag (choose about 12 from the following list). Ask your question, put your hand into the bag and pull out one or more stones. You will quickly learn the meanings and you may find that the stones talk to you and give you additional information.

You can also throw the crystals onto a 'scrying square' marked out with appropriate answers or timings.

CRYSTAL SCRYING SQUARE		
Yes	No	You would be ill-advised
Proceed with caution	Anything is possible	Create an opportunity
The time is right	You are being deceived	Hidden factors at work

Agate: *Worldly success or a pleasant surprise. Good health, wealth and long life. Particularly lucky for people connected with land.*
Amethyst: *Life changes and a shift in consciousness. Faithfulness in love, freedom from jealousy.*
Blue lace agate: *Healing is needed.*
Black agate: *Courage and prosperity.*
Red agate: *Health and longevity.*
Aventurine: *Growth and expansion possible.*

314

Bloodstone: *Unpleasant surprise.*
Clear quartz: *Permanence. Business advancement. If it loses its sparkle, betrayal.*
Citrine: *Celestial wisdom is advising you.*
Garnet: *A letter is imminent. Power and passion, good fortune and friendship, but beware strangers.*
Peridot: *Fertility or a secret admirer. If colour pales, love is fading.*
Hematite: *New opportunities await.*
Jade: *Immortality and perfection.*
Lapis lazuli: *Divine favour is yours.*
Opal: *Death or endings. If it loses its brilliance, an unfaithful lover.*
Quartz: *Be sure to clarify issues.*
Red jasper: *Pay attention to earthly affairs.*
Rose quartz: *Love and self-healing.*
Snow quartz: *Profound changes coming.*
Sapphire or blue quartz: *Truth and chastity. The past will catch up with you.*

Sardonyx: *A wedding is in the offing.*
Snowflake obsidian: *End of a challenging time.*
Tiger's eye: *Be aware that all is not as it seems.*
Topaz: *Exercise caution.*
Unakite: *Compromise and integration.*
Turquoise: *A journey is imminent.*

flower essences

Flower essences are gentle vibrational elixirs made by immersing flowers in water. They can be extremely useful for developing intuition and for enhancing protection.

Flower essences are often supplied as stock bottles that need to be diluted before use. To make a dosage bottle, put seven drops from the stock bottle into a dropper bottle filled with one third brandy to two thirds spring water. Take seven drops three times a day, before an exercise, or spray the biomagnetic field.

Flower essences for the biomagnetic field

Araryba (Araretama): *Reconstructs the biomagnetic field.*

Angelsword (Bush): *Raises vibrations.*

Fringed Violet (Bush): *Cleanses, heals and protects.*

Painini'Awa'Awa (Aloha): *Heals 'holes' in the biomagnetic field.*

Protection (Aloha), Urchin (Pacific) and Yarrow (several versions): *Protects the biomagnetic field.*

Sprays

Angel Rejuvenation (Star Flower Essences)

Biomagnetic Field Protection (Korte PHI)

Crystal Clear (Petaltone)

Orchid Essences (Living Tree)

Angel of Light (Hazel Raven)

Flower essences for the chakras

Bush Iris (Bush): *Cleanses blockages.*

Red Lily (Bush): *Cleanses root and opens crown.*

Kou (Aloha): *Stimulates brow chakra.*

Kunzite (Alaskan): *Opens higher heart.*

Fringed Violet and Flannel Flower combination (Bush): *Close down.*

Flower essences for intuitive self-contact

Bromelia 2 (Araretama)

Angelsword (Bush)

Higher Self (Korte)

Jacob's Ladder, Tundra Rose, White Violet, Brazilian Amethyst and Moldavite (Alaskan)

Nawpaka-Kahaki (Aloha)

Flower essences for channelling

Channelling (Korte)

Green Spider Orchid and Angelsword (Bush): *Distinguishes between 'good' and 'bad' channelling.*

Red Clover (FES): *Evicts an unwelcome communicator.*

Ti (Aloha and FES): *Removes spiritual possession.*

Fringed Violet and Flannel Flower (Bush): *Close down.*

Suppliers

The Flower Essence Repertoire, Living Tree: www.flowers@atlas.co.uk

David Eastoe (Petaltone and Crystal Clear): www.sacredsites.co.uk/sites/eastoe

Alaskan Flower Essences: www.alaskanessences.com

Aloha Essences: www.alohafloweressences.com

Australian Bush Essence: www.ausflowers.com.au

Flower Essence Pharmacy: www.floweressences.com

bibliography

Arberry, A.J. (trans.) *Mystical Poems of Rumi,* University of Chicago Press, 1968

Brunton, Paul, *The Secret Path,* Rider & Co., London

Chimes, Julie, *Stranger in Paradise,* Bloomsbury, London, 1996

Conze, Edward (Ed), *Buddhist Wisdom Books, The Diamond Sutra, The Wisdom Sutra,* George Allen & Unwin, London, 1958

Conze, Edward (Ed), *Buddhist Texts Through The Ages,* Bruno Cassier, Oxford, 1954

Devereux, Paul and Charla, *Lucid Dreaming,* Journey Editions, Boston, 1998

Douglas, Alfred, *Extrasensory Powers,* The Overlook Press, New York, 1976

Dychtwald, Ken, *Bodymind*

Fenwick, Peter and Elizabeth, *The Truth In The Light,* BCA, England, 1995

Green, Celia, *Lucid Dreams,* Oxford Institute of Psychophysical Research, 1968

Greenfield, Susan A., *Journey to the Centers of the Mind,* W. H. Freeman and Company, New York, 1995

Hall, Judy, *The Illustrated Guide to Divination,* Godsfield Press, New Alresford, 2000

Hall, Judy, *What's My Future?,* Penguin Books, NY, 2000

Hall, Judy, *Psychic Protection,* Thorsons, London, 1999

Hall, Judy, *The Art of Psychic Protection,* Samuel Weisers, Maine Jahn, Robert G. (Ed), *The Role of Consciousness in the Physical World,* AAAS Selected Symposium 57, Westview Press Inc, Colorado

Johnson, Raynor C., *The Imprisoned Splendour,* Hodder & Stoughton, London, 1953

Lorimar, David (Ed), *Thinking Beyond The Brain,* Floris Books, 2001

Talbot, Michael, *The Holographic Universe,* HarperCollins, London, 1996

Websites
Thinking Allowed:
www.intuition.org
Intuition in Service:
www.intuition-in-service.org,
www.princeton.edu

Karmic Readings
For details of Judy Hall's work, send an sae to her care of the publisher.

index